T0167333

BALDY

BALDY

Major General William F. Smith

GEORGE S. MAHARAY

iUniverse LLC
Bloomington

Baldy
Major General William F. Smith

Copyright © 2013 by George S. Maharay.

All rights reserved. No part of this book may be used or reproduced by any means, graphic, electronic, or mechanical, including photocopying, recording, taping or by any information storage retrieval system without the written permission of the publisher except in the case of brief quotations embodied in critical articles and reviews.

iUniverse books may be ordered through booksellers or by contacting:

iUniverse LLC
1663 Liberty Drive
Bloomington, IN 47403
www.iuniverse.com
1-800-Authors (1-800-288-4677)

Because of the dynamic nature of the Internet, any web addresses or links contained in this book may have changed since publication and may no longer be valid. The views expressed in this work are solely those of the author and do not necessarily reflect the views of the publisher, and the publisher hereby disclaims any responsibility for them.

Any people depicted in stock imagery provided by Thinkstock are models, and such images are being used for illustrative purposes only.
Certain stock imagery © Thinkstock.

ISBN: 978-1-4759-9837-5 (sc)
ISBN: 978-1-4759-9838-2 (ebk)

Library of Congress Control Number: 2013912480

Printed in the United States of America

iUniverse rev. date: 07/15/2013

CONTENTS

ILLUSTRATIONS AND MAPS

About the Author

George S. Maharay is a retired Federal executive who loves Civil War history and Vermont. His love of Civil War history is, in part, due to the fact that three of his Mother's five brothers married daughters of veterans of the Civil War

Maharay has spent over twenty five summers in Orwell, Vermont. This is his fifth book on the Civil War. Two previous books are the first written about other Vermont heroes, Major General George J. Stannard, and Major General L A. Grant. He has lectured to Civil War Round Tables and historical groups in: Vermont and has appeared in the Vermont PBS documentary, *Noble Hearts Civil War Vermont*.

ABOUT THE BOOK

Major General William F. (Baldy) Smith was a genuine, but largely unsung hero of the Civil War. After he devised and carried out the plan that saved the Army of the Cumberland at Chattanooga, General Grant said," He [Smith] is possessed of one of the clearest military minds in the army; is very practical and industrious." Grant advocated making General Smith commander of the Army of the Potomac, replacing General Meade. For a variety of reasons, that didn't happen.

General Smith was then assigned to command the Eighteenth Corps of the Army of the James under Major General Benjamin F. Butler, the man Lincoln called "The Damnedest Scoundrel". Grant expected Smith, "to keep him [Butler] straight in military matters". It was an impossible task. Butler was powerful politically, and in a presidential year, could not be controlled. Eventually, either Butler or Smith had to go, and Smith lost out.

This book is the story about the life of Major General Baldy Smith, Vermont hero.

ACKNOWLEDGEMENTS

Particular thanks are due to Paul A. Carnahan, Librarian of the Vermont Historical Society at Barre, Vermont. He preserves a treasure trove of General Smith's letters, writings, and records and made them available. Of special importance to this book are General Smith's affidavit about the Battle of Fredericksburg, (Appendix No. 2) and his letter to Senator Foot (Appendix No. 5)

Special appreciation is due the Firestone Library of Princeton University for making available General Stannard's letter to Senator Foote (sic) which is in their Andre de Copper Collection. (Appendix No. 3)

Finally, I extend many thanks to my son, C. Edward Maharay, for his excellent work in editing the book.

DEDICATION

This book is dedicated to the memory of my parents, Arthur Orr Maharay Sr. and Olive Satterly Maharay. Both loved history and instilled a love of history and respect for our heritage in their children.

INTRODUCTION

Major General William F. Smith was one of the most capable senior officers in the Union Army in the Civil War. Unfortunately, his service was hampered by ill health, his political associations and a habit of giving highly critical opinions about military affairs. In the words of Smith's best friend William B. Franklin this last practice lead to "acrimonious" relations with Smith's superiors.

James Harrison Wilson, in his 1904 biography <u>Heroes of the Great Conflict: Life and Services of William Farrar Smith, Major General, United States Volunteer in the Civil War</u>, gave the following portrait of Smith:

- "He was a strong, self-contained and deliberate in speech, and having been an industrious student and an acute thinking all his life, his opinions always commanded attention and respect.
- "A man of great purity of character and great singleness of purpose, he took an intense interest in whatever his hand found to do.
- "He was a bold and resolute thinker who indulged in no half way measures. The bolder his plans and the more dangerous his undertakings, the more careful was he in working out the details, and the more attentive was he in supervising their execution.
- "While he was austere and reserved in manners, he was most highly esteemed by all with whom he served, and received unstinted praise for his suggestions and assistance, and yet strangely enough he became involved in several notable military controversies, which so enlisted his interest and wounded his

pride as to materially change his career and cause him great unhappiness, during the later years of his life."

Wilson was a student of Smith's at West Point and later fought with Smith in both the eastern and western theaters during the Civil War. The two would remain friends until Smith's death in 1903.

A native of St. Albans, Vermont, General Smith was a member of a politically prominent family in the Green Mountain State. Intelligent, he was appointed to West Point by his uncle, Representative John Smith, a Democrat. Smith did well at the West Point, ranking fourth in the Class of 1845. His abilities were later recognized when he was assigned to teach at his alma mater in 1846 and again in 1855.

Assigned to engineering duties before the Civil War, he served in the South and while in Florida in 1855 contracted malaria. He was plagued with chills and fever for the rest of his life. During the same year he suffered from sunstroke.

Smith worked for the Light House Service, where his superior and best friend was Captain William B. Franklin, West Point, Class of 1843. At the outbreak of the Civil, Captain Smith was Engineer Secretary of the Light House Board. He volunteered his services to the governor of his native state of Vermont and was appointed colonel of the Third Regiment of Vermont volunteers.

His friend, Major General George B. McClellan, West Point Class of 1846, was made head of the Army of the Potomac in 1861. He rapidly promoted Smith to the rank of brigadier general, effective August 18, 1861, and gave him command of the First Vermont Brigade. Illness took over when Smith developed typhoid fever and he went on leave from October to December, 1861.

In May, 1862, President Abraham Lincoln permitted McClellan to establish the Fifth and Sixth Corps in the Army of the Potomac. General Franklin was named to head the Sixth Corps and Smith and his division were assigned to that corps. From then on, Franklin and Smith tented together, planned together, and fought together. To those inside and outside the army, it was always "Franklin and Smith." Baldy Smith was promoted to acting major general on July 4, 1862.

At first, Smith virtually idolized McClellan, but by the end of the Peninsular and Maryland Campaigns, he recognized the shortcomings of his friend and was openly critical of him. Yet to Lincoln and his advisors, Smith was always a McClellan protégé and Lincoln grew to despise McClellan and his cohorts and acted accordingly.

Major General Ambrose E. Burnside, West Point Class of 1847, replaced McClellan as head of the Army of the Potomac in November, 1862. Pressured into attacking Lee at Fredericksburg, Franklin and Smith offered a plan which they believed Burnside accepted. Burnside rejected their plan and had no plan at all. The result was the disastrous Battle of Fredericksburg on December 13, 1862. Franklin and Smith went out of channels and wrote directly to Lincoln implicitly criticizing Burnside and offering their plan of operations. That action was scorned. Then, with the help of the Joint Committee on the Conduct of the War, Burnside made Franklin the scapegoat for his failure at Fredericksburg. Franklin was exiled to the West and Smith lost his rank as major general.

Smith, unassigned, volunteered to help Major General Darius Couch, West Point Class of 1846, defend his native Pennsylvania in the Gettysburg Campaign. Commanding militia, Smith's troops allegedly lost a cannon that had broken down. Secretary of War Stanton and General in Chief Halleck harassed Smith about the loss, treating it as a major disaster. After Gettysburg, General Smith, with the help of prominent New Yorkers, applied for an assignment. He indicated he would serve anywhere but could not serve in the Deep South because of his history of malaria. When his assignment arrived, it was to the Gulf. It was a direct "slap-in-the-face" He then sought medical help and was able to avoid taking the assignment.

Assigned to the Army of the Cumberland as its chief engineer, Smith devised and carried out a plan that rescued that starving army when it was trapped in Chattanooga after the Battle of Chickamauga. Smith was highly praised for his work in saving the army. General Ulysses S. Grant, West Point Class of 1843, recognized Smith's capabilities, and submitted a plan of operations to Washington that Smith had prepared. Grant secured Smith's promotion to major general but had to fight to do it.

When Grant was made commander of all the armies, there was talk that he would propose Smith to be head of the Army of the Potomac. Smith was convinced that such a move would not happen because of his association with McClellan and he was right. He was then assigned as a corps commander in the Army of the James under Major General Benjamin F. Butler. There he was expected to conduct effective military operations under the militarily incompetent political general.

Temporarily assigned to the Army of the Potomac, Smith's XVIII Corps participated in the disastrous Battle of Cold Harbor on June, 1864. Smith's men, along with the rest of the Army of the Potomac, suffered tremendous losses in the fight. Smith never forgave Major General George Meade, West Point 1835, for his management of the battle.

Rushed back to the Army of the James, Smith and his corps were ordered to attack Petersburg on June 15, 1864. Smith was weak due to fever and on the day of the attack he suffered from dysentery, so badly that he could hardly stay on his horse. Initially, Smith and his men were praised for their success in the attack. Later, when it became politically or personally convenient for Grant and Butler, praise turned to blame. This latter view was the mark that prevailed.

Eventually, Butler and Smith got into a dispute and Butler, through political influence and the blackmail of Grant for his drinking, won out. Smith was so ill in early July 1864 that he had to go on leave. When he returned on July 19, Grant relieved him from duty with reasons that changed each time he voiced them. Smith spent much of the rest of his life trying to learn the real reason for his dismissal and never succeeded.

From July 1864 until December, 1864, Smith was shelved, unable to make any further contribution to the war effort. Then, on December 10, 1864, President Lincoln appointed Smith and the Honorable Henry Stansbery Special Commissioners to investigate the operations of the Military Division West of the Mississippi which General Butler had once headed. Rumor. had it that Butler and his brother had profited from illegal trade with the Confederates. The commissioner's reports were never publicized. Smith was rewarded with a brevet as major general on March 13, 1865.

In the last years of his life, the House of Representatives voted to give Smith a pension with the rank of major general The Senate cut the rank back to major, his last rank in the regular army. In 1895 the Chickamauga and Chattanooga Park Commission published an atlas that gave General William Rosecrans, West Point Class of 1842, credit for devising the plan that saved the Army of the Cumberland. Smith fought that action for six years but was unable to get the correction made (Report of a Board of Officers upon the claim of Maj. Gen William Farrar Smith. The report was dated February 1, 1901.)

CHAPTER 1

The Northern Frontier—St. Albans, Vermont

William Farrar Smith was born in St. Albans, Vermont, on February 17, 1824. (1) At that time, St. Albans was still a small village on Lake Champlain, just a few miles from the Canadian border. The Smith family migrated from Barre, Massachusetts in 1800. (2) Smith's ancestors were not new to America having played important roles in the French and Indian War and the American Revolution. (3) William Smith's parents were Ashbel, a respected farmer, and Sarah Butler Smith.

Smith's mother came from a distinguished New England family. She was a direct descendant of the Robinson family, and was thought to be a descendant of the noted Puritan clergyman, John Robinson. (4) William's uncle, John Smith, was a lawyer and a statesman. He represented St. Albans in the State Legislature from 1827 to 1833 and again from 1835 to 1837. He was elected Speaker of the Vermont House and served in that capacity from 1831 to 1833. (5) A Democrat, John Smith was elected to Congress and served one term in the House of Representatives from 1839 to 1841. His position in Congress would play an important role in William's life. John Smith's two sons were also important political figures in Vermont; John Gregory Smith was Governor of Vermont and C. Worthington Smith served in the House of Representatives. (6)

The picture that comes through of the Smith family is that they were quite religious, solid citizens, whose members believed in service to their community and their country. William F. Smith was representative of that family. A typical Vermonter, he stated his positions and his beliefs without mincing any words. One biographer, Major General

James Wilson, West Point Class of1860, wrote that General Smith "came to know by experience the dangers of frankness and friendly criticism . . ." (7)

When young Smith was thirteen, there was military action in St. Albans that must have had a profound impact upon him. (8) In 1837, French Canadian citizens in Canada revolted against the ruling British. This uprising, called the Pompineau Rebellion, led to a battle in Canada and the flight of the defeated patriots to St. Albans and Swanton in Vermont. The Canadian patriots made an attempt to return to Canada but were defeated again. As a result, they returned to the United States and remained around the Swanton area. Here they found the people of Vermont to be very sympathetic to their cause and the Vermonters openly expressed their support. Tensions between the Canadians and the Vermonters started to explode and the Canadians threatened to burn the Village of St. Albans. (9)

Officials in Washington became alarmed, and in 1838, President Van Buren sent his top military officer, General-in-Chief Winfield Scott, along with Generals Wool and Brady to restore the peace. General Wool organized a company of volunteers to deal with the problem; regulars were scarce at that time, and none were in the area. The patriots started to renew the fight only to be confronted by British Canadian troops on one side and Wool's volunteers on the other. The patriots surrendered to General Wool and the rebellion was over. (10)

Smith witnessed all of this military activity and was undoubtedly excited and impressed by it. To have the top military officer in the United States, accompanied by two of his senior officers come to the small village on the northern frontier was a rare thrill.

There can be little doubt that William F. Smith was inspired by all of these events and was enthusiastic about pursuing a career in the military. His uncle, Congressman John Smith appointed him to be a cadet at the United States Military Academy at West Point, thus starting his military career. In the summer of 1841 he would become a member of West Point's Class of 1845. (11)

Chapter 2

West Point and the Pre-War Years

William F. Smith entered the United States Military Academy at West Point as a cadet on July 1, 1841. At that time, West Point was essentially an engineering school. From its inception in 1802 until 1806, by law the superintendent was appointed from the Corps of Engineers. And, in actual practice, the superintendent continued to be selected from the Corps of Engineers from 1806 until 1866. (1) In the Civil War, key leaders on both sides were West Point graduates who had been trained as engineers, thought like engineers, and fought like engineers. Smith would follow that pattern.

Young Smith did well at the Academy, graduating fourth in a class of forty one. He did well also in his military training. He was honored by being cadet corporal, color sergeant, and lieutenant. Some of these honors were bestowed by the Commandant of Cadets, Captain Charles Smith (no relation). Commandant Smith (West Point Class of 1825) had the responsibility for military training at the Point and had the reputation of maintaining the highest standards of his profession. (2) Obviously, Cadet Smith met those standards.

While at West Point, Smith acquired the nickname of "Baldy", a sobriquet that stayed with him for the rest of his life. (3)

In the course of four years at the Military Academy, Baldy Smith came in contact with 296 cadets who graduated. There were those in his own class (1845) where the relationship was collegial; those in the classes ahead of him, (1842-1844) where his relationship to the upperclassmen he was Little Brother" to "Big Brother"; and those in the classes behind (1846-1848) where his relationship became that of "Big Brother" to "Little Brother."

With all seven classes totaling 296 men, it is safe to assume that Baldy knew all of them to some degree. In addition, as a cadet officer, he often had a supervisory role to those in his own class and to those in classes behind him.

In the Class of 1842, among those who became generals in the Civil War were: for the North, John Newton, William Rosecrans, John Pope, Seth Williams, Abner Doubleday, and George Sykes: for the South, Daniel H. Hill, Richard Anderson, James Longstreet, and Lafayette McLaws.

In the Class of 1843 were two men who would became leaders for the North; William B. Franklin and Ulysses Grant. James A. Hardie of this class would play a key role in the battle of Fredericksburg.

The Class of 1844 included Winfield Scott Hancock and Alfred Pleasanton, both who fought for the North.

In his own Class of 1845, the most notable beside himself, were Charles Stone and Fitz John Porter, both became Union Generals.

The Class of 1846 contained, for the Union; George B. McClellan, Jesse Reno, Darius Couch, and George Stoneman; for the South, Thomas "Stonewall" Jackson and George Pickett

The Class of 1847 included, for the North, Ambrose Burnside, John Gibbon, and Charles Griffin; for the South, A.P. Hill, and Henry Heth.

And in the Class of 1848 was a future Union general, John Buford.

As indicated, the classes at West Point from 1842 to 1848 were a mixture of men from the North and the South. Of those who graduated and became generals in the Civil War sixty-two percent aligned themselves with the Union while thirty-eight percent fought for the Confederacy

West Point Graduates
Who Became Generals in the Civil War (4)

Class	Union	Confederate	Total
1842	8	9	17
1843	13	3	16
1844	3	2	5
1845	9	5	14
1846	11	9	20
1847	11	2	13
1848	1	5	6
Total	**56**	**35**	**91**

Relations at West Point, along with later assignments based on their West Point records, were important factors to the men who would become generals in the Civil War. Both Union and Confederate armies were led by graduates of the U.S. Military Academy. They knew or should have known each other's strengths and weaknesses.

Erasmus D. Keyes (West Point 1832) was the only officer on the staff at West Point while Smith was a cadet there who later served in the Civil War. At that time, Keyes was a captain in the Third Artillery and an instructor of artillery at the Academy. (5) In the Civil War, Lincoln appointed Keyes, by then a major general, to head the Fourth Corps of the Army of the Potomac. The appointment was effective March 13, 1862. From that date until May 18, 1862, Smith served as a division commander under Keyes in the Peninsular Campaign.

Baldy kept a diary from October 10, 1843 to the end of 1845. On September 27, 1845 he looked back and reminisced about his days at the Point. He wrote about "my noble classmates with whom I have whiled away so many hours . . . ." The only classmate he mentioned by name was Fitz John Porter (West Point 1845). Little did he anticipate that in a few short years those noble classmates would be fighting each other, and that he and his friend Fitz John Porter would be fighting together in battles on the Peninsula and on the banks of the Antietam. (6)

Cadet Smith graduated in June 1845 and was commissioned a brevet second lieutenant in the Corps of Topographical Engineers, which at that time it was the army's most elite organization. (7)

After graduation, Lieutenant Smith made surveys of the Great Lakes, and in Texas, Arizona, Mexico, and Florida. In Texas he contracted a severe case of malaria that would plague him for the rest of his life. (8) He then worked for the Light House Service and became Engineer Secretary of its Board. He taught mathematics at West Point from 1846 to 1848, and again in 1855. His second tour at the Academy was cut short by an attack of malaria, an omen of things to come.

James Harrison Wilson in his biography of Smith wrote "The injury he received was unfortunately never entirely overcome. Throughout the whole of his subsequent life he was subject to recurrent attacks of malaria, accompanied by pain in the head with a tendency to mental depression, which disabled him entirely at times and upon one most important occasion compelled him to leave the field, when his interests and his inclinations demanded that he should remain." (9)

Smith's supervisor in the survey work was Joseph E. Johnston (West Point 1829) His supervisor and predecessor in the Light House Service was William B. Franklin (West Point 1843). He considered these two men to be his most intimate friends. (9) In the Civil War, Johnston, who was from Virginia, would join the Confederate army and lead troops against Smith on the Peninsular Campaign. Franklin, who was from Pennsylvania, would remain loyal to the Union and lead Smith and his troops in the Peninsular Campaign, the Maryland Campaign, and the Fredericksburg Campaign.

At the outbreak of the Civil War, William F. Smith was thirty seven years old, a captain in the regular army.

CHAPTER 3

Politics and Army Leadership

Politics would play a role in Smith's military career; initially favorably, and later unfavorably. In some cases, his military background and experience were the predominant factors in his leadership assignments. In others, where political factors were the major considerations; they were to his detriment.

Appointments to West Point, at that time, were made by the president and Members of Congress. Politics played a role in many cases, not all, in selecting candidates to enter that honored institution. Smith's entrance into the military service was based on politics. As indicated earlier, he was a Democrat and was appointed to the United States Military Academy by his uncle, Representative John Smith of Vermont who was a Democrat (1)

Smith's close friend, William B. Franklin, a Democrat, was appointed to West Point by Senator James Buchanan, a Democrat (2). George B. McClellan (West Point 1846) who would become a Democrat, was appointed to the Wet Point by President John Tyler, a Whig (3) George G. Meade (West Point 1835) and of no known political affiliation, was appointed to the Academy by President Andrew Jackson, a Democrat. (4) And Ulysses S. Grant (West Point1843) a Whig, was appointed to the Academy by Representative Thomas Hamer, a Democrat (6). In all of these cases, the men were appointed on the basis of an appeal of a parent to a member of Congress or a president.

With the advent of the Civil War, the Union army was almost entirely made up of volunteers in regiments raised by the states. The governors controlled appointments in these organizations leaving few appointments to leadership positions to be made by the War Department or the president. Officers in the regular army and persons who had military training and experience had to look to governors for promotions or appointments to leadership assignments.

Baldly Smith's promotion from a captain in the regular army to colonel of the Third Vermont was made by Governor Erastus Fairbanks of Vermont, a Republican. (6)

Franklin was one of the few who were promoted in the regular army. With the outbreak of the war, the army had to be reorganized. President Lincoln gave the assignment to develop a plan to Secretary of Treasury Chase (Secretary of War Cameron was preoccupied with buying arms and ammunition). Lincoln also personally appointed a three man committee of military officers to advise Chase; one of whom was Smith's friend, Captain Franklin. The committee recommended an expansion of the regular army and Franklin was then assigned to command the new Twelfth United States Regiment and was promoted to colonel on May 14, 1861. (7)

George B. McClellan was sought after by the governors of Ohio, Pennsylvania, and New York based on his military background. His first offer, which he accepted, was made by Governor William Dennison of Ohio, a Republican. He was appointed major general of volunteers on April 23, 1861 and given command of Ohio troops. (8)

U.S. Grant, then a civilian, offered his services to the War Department on May 24, 1861 and his letter was pigeon-holed. He assisted in organizing regiments in Missouri and Illinois and was appointed mustering officer for the State of Illinois. Governor Richard Yates of that state, a Republican, appointed him colonel of the 21st Illinois Volunteer Regiment on June 17, 1861. (9)

Once in a leadership position, the attitudes of officers in the army regarding politics were unusual and difficult to comprehend if one applies today's standards. Many continued to mix politics and military service. There was an historical precedent for this. In 1852, Winfield Scott ran for president on the Whig ticket while serving as general-in-chief of the army. He continued to serve as general-in-chief until October 30, 1861. Other leaders would follow Scott's example.

Major General George B. McClellan was called to Washington on July 27, 1861 to assume command of what would become the Army of the Potomac. He felt free to offer advice to the president, advice that went beyond military matters. On August 4, 1861, he sent a memo to the president that was both an advocacy of a political approach to the war and a proposal on military strategy. (10) Later, in July, 1862, despite his failure on the Peninsula, he handed Lincoln the famed "Harrison's Landing letter" which has been described as a "Democratic Manifesto." And still later, after the Battle of Antietam, he drafted a letter to President Lincoln objecting the president's preliminary Emancipation Proclamation. When his officers convinced him not to send the letter, he then issued an order to his troops with a line in it that read," The remedy for political errors, if any are committed, is to be found only in the action of the people at the polls."(11) With the mid-term elections coming in November, this was an invitation to the soldiers (and their friends and relatives) to vote against the administration.

Baldy Smith's classmate, Major General Fitz John Porter, was so incensed about Lincoln's preliminary Emancipation Proclamation that he wrote to the editor of the Administration's chief opposition newspaper, the New York World, saying the soldiers were, ". . . upset by the absurd proclamation of a political coward". (12)

Officers had no hesitation in contacting members of Congress. Brigadier General Charles Hamilton wrote to congressmen after the fighting at Yorktown in 1862 criticizing McClellan. (13) Many others contacted lawmakers to advance their cause. Finally, on March 30, 1864, Grant issued General Orders No. 129 and stopped these attempts by senior officers from seeking help from their friends in Congress.

Officers also criticized Congress. When the Joint Committee on the Conduct of the War issued a report blaming Franklin for the failure at Fredericksburg, he promptly wrote a pamphlet refuting the Committee's allegation. With the aid of General Smith and others, he sent a thousand copies of his pamphlet to "certain congressmen, newspapers, and other men of influence."(14)

Lincoln and his administration were keenly aware of the political views of the senior officer in the army and were prone to seek the help of those who were supportive of their actions. The importance of this was reflected in their evaluations of officers. As an example, on March 26, 1864, Lincoln met with Halleck, Stanton, and Grant. Two of the most important leaders that affected Smith's service were Ambrose Burnside and Benjamin Butler. Burnside was judged to be "competent under someone else's orders" and he was "politically important". (15) Butler (and Nathaniel Banks) were deemed to be "dubious commanders . . . . but both had an importance beyond the downright military." Butler was politically important and "used" by the Administration. (16)

Lincoln and Stanton were also prone to punish the senior officers in the army who actively opposed to the administration's policies or actions. The relief of McClellan and the court-martial Porter are examples.

Such was the environment that senior military encountered in the Civil War. General Smith was ill-suited to operate in such an environment. He was a trained military officer who saw things clearly and called them as he saw them. He would pay the price for doing so as the leadership of the army changed to reflect Lincoln's goals.

CHAPTER 4

The Beginning of the Civil War

At the start of 1861, tensions between North and South were bubbling over. All attempts at a peaceful settlement were failing. War was just a few months away.

In February, 1861, John A. Dix, a Northerner replaced Howell Cobb (later a Confederate general) as Secretary of the Treasury, Dix became an instant hero in the North when he issued an order to protect the flag on the New Orleans Customs House that said, "If anyone attempts to haul down the American flag, shoot him on the spot." (1)

Captain Smith knew that the lighthouses on the Florida Keys were vital to Northern shipping and might be possible targets for Southern sympathizers if a war broke out. He was acquainted with Secretary Dix from his work with the Light House Board, which was part of Treasury. Smith sought the Secretary's permission to get rid of light house keepers who were sympathetic to the Southern Cause and to take arms and ammunition there to protect the important lights. He was successful in his quest and the lights remained in Northern hands and guided shipping in that area throughout the war. (2)

When Smith returned from Florida he was sent to New York City to muster in volunteers. Then, he spent a brief tour of duty with General Benjamin Butler at Fortress Monroe. After that assignment, he was sent to be on the staff of General Irwin McDowell (West Point 1838) but did not participate in the First Battle of Bull Run. (3)

Captain Smith recognized that if he were to get a promotion, as other West Pointers had done, he would have to get it through the governor of a state. In April he married Miss Sarah Ward Lyon, a daughter of Samuel Lyon, a New York lawyer. While on his honeymoon he offered his services to Governor Erasmus Fairbanks of his native state Vermont.

Fairbanks readily accepted Smith's offer, but Smith had to be released from the regular army before he could be appointed as a volunteer. The War Department refused to release him, doing so several times. Finally, General-in-Chief Winfield Scott intervened and Captain Smith was commissioned colonel of the Third Vermont Regiment. This was in the last week of July. The commission was backdated to April 27 so that Smith would outrank Colonel Henry Whiting of the Second Vermont (West Point 1845) who was not a native Vermonter. (4)

He was now Colonel Smith. His new regiment had been mustered into federal service on July 16 and sent to Washington where it arrived on July 26. Smith followed and assumed command in August. (5) The regiment was stationed in Virginia at the end of the Chain Bridge over the Potomac River.

After the First Battle of Bull Run, McDowell was quickly replaced by Major General George B McClellan, who was given command of all the Union forces around Washington. He and Smith had been friends at West Point and McClellan promptly promoted Smith to brigadier general effective August 13, 1861. (6) Smith then asked for a brigade of Vermont troops, and was given the Second, Third, Fourth and Fifth Vermont. The brigade, known as the First Vermont Brigade, shows up on McClellan's organization chart of October 15, 1861. (7) The brigade was one of the best in the Army of the Potomac and Smith proudly followed its achievements throughout the war. (8)

The months from October 1861 to March 1862 were spent organizing the army and drilling the men. Smith sent Brigadier General Winfield Hancock and 5,000 men to surprise the Rebels and capture them and occupy Munson's Hill. The expedition ended when Hancock found that the Confederates had left before he and his men got there. (9)

The single major military event to occur around Washington in the fall of 1861 was the Battle of Ball's Bluff. McClellan ordered Smith's classmate, Brigadier General Charles Stone to determine whether or not the Confederates had left Dranesvillle on the Virginia side of the Upper Potomac. McClellan suggested that Stone make a slight demonstration. (10) Stone's subordinate, Colonel Edward Baker, a former senator and friend of Lincoln, impetuously attacked the Rebels who were in a strong defensive position at Ball's Bluff. Baker was killed in the action, one of 921 Union casualties in the disastrous attack. (11)

Ball's Bluff started a precedent for subsequent Union failures. <u>For a Union loss, there must be a scapegoat.</u> Stone was blamed for Ball's Bluff even though McClellan and others knew he was not responsible for the disaster. Stone was targeted by powerful men in the Senate and in the North because they deemed him to be pro-slavery He was arrested and jailed for 189 days but never charged. His military career was ruined. (12)

In December, 1861, General McClellan became ill with typhoid fever. The Joint Committee on the Conduct of the War was formed on December 10. Its purpose, initially, was to get McClellan to act. McClellan was invited to be the first to testify on December 23 but when the date arrived he was too ill to do so.

General Franklin was the first to appear before the Committee and he testified on December 26. The Committee wanted to know if Franklin knew McClellan's plans. Franklin said that he did but felt that he could not divulge them. Upon leaving the Committee, Franklin went directly to McClellan's home. There he met Baldy Smith who had just visited the Young Napoleon and who advised Franklin that the general was too ill to have more visitors. (13)

In January1862, McClellan shared the details of his plans for the coming campaign with Franklin, Smith and Fitz John Porter. These three were his intimate friends and advisers. (14)

With McClellan ill and no action being taken to attack the Confederates at Manassas Junction, Lincoln decided to take matters into his own hands. He held meetings with his top military men and members of his cabinet. On Monday, January 13, he held another meeting which McClellan was able to attend. Secretaries Chase and Seward, Generals McDowell, Franklin, and Meigs (West Point 1836) were present. The President called on McDowell and Franklin to review the military options. Following McDowell's presentation, Franklin stated that he agreed with McClellan's plan. McDowell, who was supposed to be McClellan's second in command, quickly remarked "that he was unaware of any plan of General McClellan." (15) McClellan had shared his plans with his advisers only.

On March 8, 1862, Lincoln met with twelve senior officers of the Army of the Potomac. He required them to vote on McClellan's proposed plans for the army. They voted eight to four to approve it. Franklin and Smith were for the plan, Generals McDowell, Edwin Sumner, and Samuel Heintzelman (West Point 1826) opposed it. Keyes voted for the plan with reservations. Lincoln asked the officers opinions about organizing the army by corps. All supported the proposal. He then organized the Army of the Potomac into five corps and named the corps commanders. All this was done without McClellan's involvement or approval. Lincoln appointed Irwin McDowell to command the First Corps; Edwin Sumner, the Second; Samuel Heintzelman, the Third; Erasmus Keyes, the Fourth, and Nathaniel Banks, the Fifth. Dissent in the leadership of the Army of the Potomac was almost guaranteed with these actions.

Baldy Smith was extremely critical of these appointments. He was certain that Secretary of War Stanton was responsible for them and that they were based solely on seniority. He wrote "General McDowell was vain and arrogant man hounded by the defeat at Bull Run, which had caused McClellan to supersede him. Who never accepted the situation his defeat the Bull Run naturally brought him to and began at once *after General McClellan in the kindness and weakness of his he asked for his appointment as Major General of Volunteers and obtained it,* to work for an independent command. The three others had no claim to their positions except by seniority and senility. Old officers of the Regular Army, their services had been honorable enough; but without military reading they were too old to develop into anything beyond martinets, and never grasped the situation in any battle in which they were ever engaged." (16) McDowell was 44 years old, Sumner, 64, Heintzelman, 55, and Keyes, 51. In contrast, McClellan, Porter, Franklin and Smith were all in their late thirties at the time.

Smith and his division were assigned to Keyes's Fourth Corps. He and his command would soon experience the incompetence of their leaders.

CHAPTER 5

The Peninsular Campaign—Lee's Mill

General Gorge B. McClellan moved the Army of the Potomac from its base in Washington to Fortress Monroe from March1 17 to April 2, 1862. This was the start of the Peninsular Campaign.

Baldy Smith had high hopes for the Young Napoleon. He wrote, "At this period, I was devoted to the General and imagined he was the providential leader who was going to give us a speedy termination of the war. With a long intimacy, warm personal friendship, and my partisan character, I began the campaign with the most sanguine hopes of making for himself a name among the captains of the world." Then he added," Between Yorktown and Harrison's Landing on the James river, where we took shelter *from a retreating army*, all this was beaten out of me, and my reason which never blinded me to weakness when it was shown, made for me at the end of the campaign a different picture of my demi-god from one made at the outset of the war." (1)

Smith continued his comments on McClellan, "Starting out on an offensive campaign of his own planning, he never could make his mind to bring on a decisive engagement, and allowed the enemy to concentrate and assail him. He was moreover not sufficiently quick on expedients, and when a part of the force he expected to have (McDowell's command) was taken from him he had no other plan to adopt, and was detained by obstacles, that many a man of his ability would have brushed aside." (2)

Smith's analysis of his friend's character explains why the Peninsular Campaign failed. McClellan had a single plan, i.e. to conduct a siege, he planned no other option. He couldn't adjust to change. In all his actions,

15

his primary concern was to save his army. These factors dominated the entire campaign.

McClellan's plan was based upon having 155,000 men. (3). He wrote, "I had hoped, let me say, by rapid movements, to drive before me or capture the enemy on the Peninsula, open the James river, and press on to Richmond before he should be materially reinforced from other parts of the territory", (4) The plan was based upon the assumption that the Navy would assist on both the James and York Rivers. (5) Yet McClellan knew before he left Washington that the Navy could not help him, "so he went fully prepared for siege operations." (6).

McClellan's philosophy in campaigning was revealed when he told Secretary of War Stanton that he planned to win by strategy and not by fighting. (7) To his troops, he said," I am to watch over you as a parent to his children (8) it shall be my care . . . . to gain success with the least possible loss" (9) He limited his actions by this approach.

On March 27 Heintzelman and his Third Corps were the first to arrive at Fortress Monroe. He reported that he found only a small force of Confederates in the area and proposed to attack them. McClellan responded the next day cautioning Heintzelman not to advance because it might "prematurely develop our plans to the enemy."(10) McClellan personally arrived at Fortress Monroe on April 2,

On April 4, McClellan was notified that McDowell's First Corps was changed to the Department of the Rappahannock and was being held back to defend Washington. In addition, Bank's Fifth Corps was renamed the Department of the Shenandoah and was assigned the task of dealing with Stonewall Jackson in the Valley (11) Three days later McClellan ordered the siege. (12) He then named his close friend and adviser, Brigadier General Fitz John Porter, director of the siege. (13) In doing so he bypassed the corps commander, Heintzelman, and ignored the corps structure that President Lincoln had established.

Major General John Magruder, CSA (West Point 1830) defended the Lower Peninsula. He had strong fortifications at Yorktown and he had dammed the Warwick River, but he had to defend the area from Yorktown to the James River and he had only a few men to face McClellan's horde. He wrote, "I was compelled to place at Gloucester, Yorktown, and Mulberry Island fixed garrisons amounting to 6000 men, my whole force being 11,000, so that it will be seen that the balance of the line embracing a length of 13 miles was defended by about 5000 men." (14)

In his report, Magruder noted that ". . . . Dam No.1, the center of our line, was the weakest point in it" [the Confederate defense]. He also wrote." . . . . to my utter surprise, he [McClellan] permitted day after day to elapse without an assault." (15)

The Union forces moved up the Peninsula from Fortress Monroe in two columns. Smith led the left column. The march started on April 4 and on April 5, Baldy and his men reached Dam No. 1 and Lee's Mill. He stated, "Knowing General Keyes to be irresolute and afraid of responsibility, I took it upon myself to give (Brigadier General Winfield S.) Hancock orders to take his brigade up the creek in the early morning on a reconnaissance, and if he could find a place where he could force it, to hold it and send word to me and I would at once march to his aid with the other brigades of the division." Smith then went to General Keyes' headquarters to report his action. There he learned that Keyes had received orders from McClellan ". . . . not to undertake any offensive operations until the line had been thoroughly examined by engineers." Hancock had found a place at Dam No. 1 where he could cross the river but to his dismay was ordered to return to camp. (16)

Finally, on April 15, Smith received orders from McClellan to see if he could interrupt work by the Confederates who were strengthening their defenses at Dam No. 1. After getting his brigades and artillery in position, Smith sent four companies of his old regiment, the Third Vermont, "to cross the river and feel the enemy." The Vermonters were driven back with significant losses. (17) That was the extent of assaults on the Warwick line. General McClellan issued orders ". . . not bring on a general engagement." (18)

At Lee's Mill the first of several controversies about General Smith reared its ugly head. He was accused of being drunk during the reconnaissance. According to his detractors, this was the reason, widely circulated, for his alleged failure to support the Third Vermont. Smith stated that he was thrown from his horse while going at full speed "which gave me such a shock that I was partially dazed for the remainder of the fight." (19) A resolution containing the accusation was presented in Congress and Smith immediately called for a court of inquiry. Most of the field officers (major and above) and all of the colonels in the Vermont Brigade called the allegation "unequivocally false." McClellan dismissed the idea of a court of inquiry based on lack of evidence. A committee from the U.S. Senate visited the camps near Lee's Mill and reported "the charge against General Smith to be without foundation," (20) That was the end of the first controversy.

On May 4, Smith learned that the Rebels had abandoned the Warwick line. They did so when Smith's friend Confederate General Johnston (West Point 1829) found that the "Union batteries [at Yorktown] were nearly ready." He issued orders to his troops to move towards Williamsburg. (21) The Army of the Potomac followed.

CHAPTER 6

The Battle of Williamsburg

When Baldy Smith learned of the Rebel retreat, he started his division in the pursuit. George Benedict, the Vermont historian, wrote, "the next day, May 5ᵗʰ, the planless and unsatisfactory Battle of Williamsburg was fought." (1)

Two Union columns moved inland. The column on the left went from Lee's Mill to Williamsburg and was led by Smith and his division. Joseph Hooker (West Point 1837) and his division had the lead on a parallel road to the right, the road from Yorktown to Williamsburg, The two forces met before they reached Williamsburg and Smith assumed the lead. Hooker, impetuous, asked General Sumner, the senior commander on the field, for permission to move to the left and take the advance. Sumner agreed. (2)

Magruder had constructed a line of forts about two miles in front of Williamsburg, the largest of which was Fort Magruder. That fort was on the Union left in Hooker's front. (3) Upon arriving at the fortifications, Hooker, without orders, attacked certain that he would be supported. (4) He committed the Union forces to a battle on his own.

Shortly after daybreak on May 5, "an old Negro" appeared at Smith's position and said that there was a road leading to Rebel forts that was not occupied and behind Fort Magruder. (5) General Smith sent a member of his staff with the man and verified his report. Smith then went to General Sumner to get permission to advance his command and take the unoccupied defenses. Sumner gave Smith permission to "send one brigade to the first fort, but no further." Smith sarcastically wrote later," I left General Sumner with a feeling of admiration for the old plantation Negro who had shown more knowledge of strategy than the second officer in the Army of the Potomac." (6) The next hours were among the most frustrating in Smith's entire military career. Following Sumner's restrictive orders, Smith sent Hancock and his brigade to capture the unoccupied forts. Despite Sumner's limitations, Smith told Hancock to go as far as he could, and if needed, he would reinforce him. Hancock turned the enemy's flank and called for support to protect his rear.

On the Union left, Hooker was successful at first, and then was attacked and needed help. Sumner ordered Smith to send a brigade to Hooker. Smith persuaded Sumner to change his order and received permission to support Hancock, only to have that order rescinded. Benedict wrote in *Vermont in the Civil War*, "Again General Smith asked permission to go to Hancock's aid. . . . . Finally, Sumner not only refused to permit Smith to send any more troops to the right, but he ordered Hancock back to his first position." (7) The Confederates attacked Hancock and he repulsed them but was not strong enough to go forward. The opportunity was lost.

All day long Smith sent messages to General McClellan begging him to come on to the field. McClellan finally arrived around 5:00 P.M. but it was too late to organize an assault. The wily General Johnston retreated that night.

Two days after the Battle of Williamsburg, General McClellan complained about the leadership of his corps commanders in the battle and requested Secretary of War Stanton to permit him to return to a division structure for the Army of the Potomac. He wanted authority "to relieve from duty with his army, commanders of corps or divisions who found themselves incompetent. (8) It was clear that he wanted to get rid of the corps structure and the corps commanders.

McClellan had already cashiered Brigadier Charles Hamilton a division commander in Heintzelman's Third Corps. The alleged reason was incompetence. The real offense was writing, not fighting. Hamilton had written Members of Congress complaining about McClellan's leadership. "Little Mac" would not tolerate criticism, particularly to Members of Congress. Hamilton's removal created uproar on the part of the Congressman and Senators. Lincoln had his hands full dealing with their complaints. For his part, McClellan refused to budge.

Lincoln sent a private letter to McClellan in which he wrote, "Are you strong enough—even with my help that you can set your foot on the necks of Sumner, Heintzelman, and Keyes all at once?" (9) He continued saying that McClellan's struggle against the corps commanders was seen as an effort to pamper one or two of his pets and that McClellan only consulted with Fitz John Porter and Franklin. (10) He could have added Baldy Smith.

Finally, on May 18, Lincoln appeased the petulant Young Napoleon. He consented to the establishment of the Fifth and Sixth Provisional Corps and the appointment of Porter and Franklin to head them. (11)

Baldy Smith and his division were transferred to the new Sixth Corp under General Franklin. Smith was delighted. He wrote," I had an old friend, a man of great ability for my immediate commander. During all the times we were together up to the time General Franklin was relieved (May 18, 1862-February 6, 1863) after the campaign of [General Ambrose E.] Burnside, we had the same headquarters, the same tent and had a common mess and there was never the slightest disagreement between us as to plans and details. We worked harmoniously for the same end and with unparalleled serenity. Matters were discussed between us, and a conclusion arrived at and there was nothing more to be said. We generally saw things with the same lights, and when we did not he was the superior office, and in that way thing was settled" (12)

CHAPTER 7

Lee Takes Command

After Williamsburg, the Army of the Potomac moved slowly toward Richmond. As McClellan's juggernaut neared the Confederate capital, President Jefferson Davis (West Point 1828) held a meeting on May 15 to discuss the evacuation of Richmond. General Robert E. Lee (West Point 1829) Davis' military adviser was adamantly opposed to any such action. (1) Then Davis decided to take the initiative. Historian Clifford Dowdey wrote, "On May 31 President Davis forced General Johnston to leave his entrenchments and attack McClellan." (2) The Battle of Seven Pines or Fair Oaks began.

Late in the first day of the battle, May 31 Johnston, one of Baldy Smith's best friends in the old army, was severely wounded. Davis appointed Lee to replace him as commander of the Army of Northern Virginia on June 2. (3) (4) This was the most important leadership change in the Civil War. McClellan had served under Lee in the Mexican War (5) and was certain that he understood him. He described Lee as "too cautious and weak under grave responsibility . . . . and likely to be timid & irresolute in action." (6) He could not have been more wrong. Baldy Smith highlighted this flaw in The Young Napoleon when he wrote in his autobiography "General McClellan was no judge of character—a very important weakness in a public man, and an especial failing in a commanding general." (7)

The Confederate attack at Seven Pines was repulsed. After that the two armies spent the month of June moving into position. Lee's strategy was "to concentrate for an attack at a point of his selection rather than to wait on the enemy's initiative." (8) He followed that strategy in June,

1862 and adhered to it until after the Battle of the Wilderness in 1864. In the meantime, McClellan spent June in preparing for the siege of Richmond.

General Fitz John Porter and his Fifth Corps and George McCall (West Point 1822) and his division were on the north side of the Chickahominy River where they were separated from the main body of the Army of the Potomac. Porter wrote, "McClellan had been forced in this position on the Chickahominy and held there by the oft-repeated assurances that McDowell's Corps of 40,000 men, then at Fredericksburg, would be advanced to Richmond and formed on his immediate right, which would make that wing safe." Porter supports this assertion by citing a letter from Secretary of War Stanton to McClellan dated June 18 in which Stanton said, "You are instructed to cooperate so as to establish this communication [with McDowell] as soon as possible, by extending your right wing to the north of Richmond." (9)

Baldy Smith recognized the weakness of Porter's position and offered a solution. He wrote, "Shortly after that I was sent across the Chickahominy, [south of it] and took up a position at Golding's Farm with my right resting on the stream, and here came another period of inaction. On the 24th of June, I asked General McClellan to come to my front, and took him out to the picket line, and showed him the country, an old tavern in the distance (the key of the position) and assuring him that by a rapid march we could capture that point and thus be on vantage ground, stipulating only that he should see that when we began the fight there should be a cordial and hearty cooperation from our left. To this he assented, saying, however, that he wished his reserve artillery to have a chance to distinguish themselves, and that I must go to work that night, and dig an epaulement [on Garnett Hill in front of the Federal lines on Golding's Farm] for the guns which should be in place by daylight . . . . Colonel [Barton S] Alexander of the engineers that night constructed a breastwork so quietly that it was unknown to the enemy till daylight. During the night, however, a note came from the General postponing the movement till the next night; and the next night I received an order from him to do nothing to bring on a general engagement." (10)

"The next day [General Robert E] Lee's movement developed which began the fighting [Battle of Mechanicsville, June 26, 1862] on his plans rather than ours. That night—the 26 about midnight—the

General passed by our headquarters on the way to [General Fitz John] Porter, who was concentrating to fight the battle of Gaines' Mill [June 27, 1862]. General Franklin and I urged him to withdraw all the troops from the north bank of the river destroying the bridges and leave the tired troops to watch the river while we who were fresh should attack in force, and could beat Lee's army there and capture Richmond before Lee could make the long detour by Mechanicsville to later push in the battle. This was not done." (11)

After the war was over, Generals Smith and Johnston discussed Lee's attack at Gaines' Mill. Johnston felt that Lee had made a mistake, and McClellan didn't take advantage of the opportunity. General Johnston agreed with Smith and Franklin that they had been right in their assessment of the situation. (12)

About 2:00 P.M. on June 27 Lee attacked Porter and his isolated corps at Gaines's Mill. Initially, Lee's force consisted of Longstreet, A. P, Hill and D. H. Hill. Stonewall Jackson joined the fray around 4:00 P.M. (13) At about 4:00 P.M. Henry Slocum's (West Point 1852) division of the Sixth Corps was sent across the Chickahominy River to support Porter. Repeated Rebel attacks broke Porter's line at the end of the day and forced him to retreat and leave the field. (14)

General Smith could see part of the battlefield from his vantage point on Golding's Farm, but he was essentially a spectator. The siege artillery which McClellan had sent to him did help break some of the Confederate attacks. (15) Late in the day, Toombs Georgians attacked Smith's position. Hancock, with his brigade and help from the Fourth and Sixth Vermont drove them back. (16) That was the extent of General Smith's involvement in the battle on June 27.

McClellan decided to change his base from White House on the Pamunkey River to the James River, where the Navy could support him. The first record about this change of base is in McClellan's report of July 15, 1862. He wrote that on June 24 he learned that Confederate Generals Stonewall Jackson, Richard Ewell (West Point 1840) and William Whiting (West Point 1845) were preparing to attack his right flank and "cut off our communications with the White House, and throw the right wing of our army into the Chickahominy." He continued, "Fortunately, I had a few days before provided against this contingency, by ordering a number of transports to the James River, loaded with commissary, quartermaster, and ordnance supplies. (17)

Porter stated in his report that he met with General McClellan on June 26, the day before the Battle of Gaines' Mill. At that time, McClellan and Porter learned that Jackson was on the field and was moving to a position where he could flank McClellan's right. Porter wrote, "It was thus rendered necessary to select which side of the Chickahominy should be held in force, there being on each side an army of our enemies equivalent (in connection with their breastworks) to the whole of our army, and these two armies and defenses well connected with each other and with Richmond, their base.." (18) McClellan and his generals assumed that Lee's strength was twice theirs. Contemporary estimates were that McClellan had 92,500 men and Lee had 80,726, including Jackson's men. (19)

After the Battle of Gaines's Mill, McClellan met with his corps commanders or their representatives. Porter wrote ". . . I was then instructed to withdraw to the South side of the river and destroy the bridges after me." (20) The retreat was on. At the same meeting General McClellan ordered the change of base. This involved moving the army and its supplies from White House on the Pamunkey River to Harrison's Landing on the James River. The army and the supplies and equipment had to cross White Oak Swamp to get to the James. Involved in the move were an army of about 92,500 men, (21) 4,000 wagons, (22) 2,500 beef cattle, and both field and siege artillery. (23) Materials at the White House Depot and at Savage's Station that could not be moved were destroyed. Locomotives and railroad cars on the Richmond and York Railroad were also destroyed. At the field hospital at Savage's Station were 2,500 wounded; these men were left to become Rebel prisoners. (24)

McClellan started the move to the James the night of June 27. It wasn't until sometime on June 29 that Lee fully realized that the Army of the Potomac was changing its base. (25) (26)

Chapter 8

Covering the Retreat to the James

In the morning of June 28 General Smith received preliminary orders to command the rear guard of the retreating army. He prepared for the movement by changing his front so that his entire division faced the enemy across the Chickahominy River. Smith wrote "Since the night when I was making preparations for my attack. I had not an hour's rest but the labors and excitement carried me through very well, and there was much to do to keep away sleep." (1) Smith turned for help to the lumbermen in the division, expert axe-men from Maine, Vermont, and Wisconsin. These hardy outdoorsmen quickly cut down the forest in Smith's front opening his view to the Chickahominy. (2)

Smith waited for final orders during the night of June 28 in a state of "terrible anxiety". He was convinced that the Confederates were on his flank and in his front in numbers that would overwhelm him. (3)

General Robert E. Lee was also convinced that his forces could destroy Smith's division. Impatient, he sent an unusually curt message to General Magruder on June 29 "I regret much that you have made so little progress in pursuit of the enemy . . . . we must lose no more time or he will escape up entirely." (4)

Smith's orders finally arrived on the morning of June 29 and he moved to a designated position near Savage's Station. He had been told that he would find Slocum's division of the Sixth Corps on his right and Sumner and his Second Corps on his left. (5) Neither was there. Slocum reported that ". . . at Savage's Station about 5:00 A.M. Sunday I received orders from General McClellan in person to move the division across

White Oak Swamp."(6) McClellan had bypassed Franklin who was left unaware of his subordinate's departure.

Sumner had been attacked near Fair Oaks and had beaten the attack back. He refused to leave that position and remained there until Generals Franklin and Smith convinced him that General McClellan had issued orders for his withdrawal to Savage's Station. (7) (8) General Heintzelman and his Third Corps were also supposed to be at Savage's Station but Heintzelman decided that the area was too crowded and left on his own. (9) McClellan's plans had called for three corps being at Savage's Station but, in reality, only one and one half remained there. Worse yet, McClellan left the area and went on a gunboat on the James. Three battles would be fought without his leadership

While Sumner and his Second Corps held Savage's Station, Baldy Smith and his men started towards White Oak Swamp. About 4:00 P.M., on June 29 rebel artillery and infantry advanced on the railroad toward Sumner's position. Smith was about a mile away and was called back to enter the fight. The fighting continued until after dark when Magruder's attacks were finally rebuffed. (10)

The night march to White Oak Swamp started at 10:00 P.M. on June 29 and ended around 5:00 A.M. the next day. The trek tested everyone's endurance. The experience of the First Vermont Brigade, a part of Smith's division, illustrated the problems with the march. ". . . . .the road was filled with wagons, ambulances, and artillery mingled with the troops. Throngs of stragglers, of other organizations, hung upon the rear of the brigade and it was with difficulty that any organization was preserved. All night long the march continued." (11)

General Smith remained at the bridge over a stream in the Swamp cheering his men until all had crossed. He then destroyed the bridge and had his men take their assigned positions on the south side of the stream. Smith soon received orders from General McClellan "to hold that position at all hazards till relieved by an order from him." (12) The position was essential to transfer of the army and all of its supplies and equipment to the new base on the James. It had to be held if McClellan were to save his army. (13)

After making his dispositions for his division, an exhausted Baldy Smith wrote "I threw myself on the ground and tried to get some sleep." (14)

The effort was not successful as the enemy was nearby. Stonewall Jackson arrived in the vicinity of White Oak Swamp about noon. As he positioned his artillery, his actions were sheltered from the sight of Smith's division by woods. Then, in early afternoon, thirty Confederate guns erupted. General Franklin later commented about the barrage "It commenced with a severity I never heard equaled in the war." (15)

The Confederates assumed that they had driven Smith and his division from the field but they were wrong. After the initial blast, Confederate General D.H. Hill, a division commander in Jackson's command, said they found that the Union "battery had taken up a position behind a point of woods, where it was perfectly sheltered from our guns, but could play upon the broken bridge and ford, and every part of the uncultivated field." (16)

After the initial bombardment, General Franklin said "The enemy kept up firing during the whole day and crossed [the swamp with] some infantry below our position, but made no very serious attempt to cross during the day but contented himself with the cannonading and the firing of sharpshooters." (17)

General D.H. Hill indicated that Confederate cavalry found a ford that was "perfectly practicable for infantry." Jackson ignored the finding and remained where he was, satisfied with the work of his artillery and riflemen. As a result, five Confederate divisions remained inactive the afternoon and evening of June 30. (18)

One of General Smith's staff officers found a road that went to the James River that the troops could use. It was sheltered from the Rebel troops under Generals James Longstreet and A.P. Hill who had earlier attempted to break the Union line that protected the retreating army. About 10:00 P.M., after the trains, troops, and artillery had moved on, Smith's division marched toward Malvern Hill. (19)

With another tiring night march, the division reached Malvern Hill where the Confederates attacked and were severely beaten on July 1. Smith's division was on hand but was not engaged in the fight. Porter's Fifth Corps led the Union defense at Malvern Hill where the Confederates suffered terrible losses, some 4,150 casualties. (20) They left the field and started retreating toward Richmond.

At daylight on July 2 General Fitz Porter, riding at the head of his corps, met his West Point classmate Baldy Smith at the junction of two roads leading to Harrison's Landing. The two dismounted and started talking. Both officers were physically dead tired. Porter was also disconsolate. He described the Battle of Malvern Hill and the Rebel retreat. Then, at the end of the battle, he had sought out McClellan who was on a Navy gunboat in the James River. Porter was McClellan's most trusted subordinate and held great sway with the commander. That night, Porter pleaded with McClellan to follow the retreating Rebels and destroy them. Hours of persuasive argument went for naught. McClellan refused to budge. (21) (22)

Later General Smith learned from Confederate General Joseph E. Johnston that Lee's army had been in such disarray that the Army of the Potomac could easily have marched into Richmond. General John Reynolds (West Point 1841) was a prisoner in Libby Prison in Richmond at the time and his captors, Southern West Pointers whom Reynolds had known before the war, confirmed Johnston's assessment. (23)

The camp at Harrison's Landing was in a low spot with one road in and out. Jeb Stuart arrived at the heights above the camp and fired artillery into it. McClellan ordered Smith to drive Stuart off, which he did. Smith had recognized the vulnerability of the army in that location and critically asked the adjutant of the army "who has selected such a place of defense of the army?" When told that General McClellan had selected the place, Smith voiced his opinion and it was not a positive one. (24)

Later Smith requested that the other division of the Sixth Corps, Slocum's, be sent to him and it soon joined him. He also asked General Franklin to tell McClellan that the plateau was the place for the whole army. Smith. wrote [then] "Jackson came along, and tried the line through its whole length, and abandoned any idea of an attack upon us." (25)

At the end of the Peninsular Campaign, Baldy Smith's attitude toward General McClellan had gone from adulation to one of bitter disappointment.

CHAPTER 9

Between Campaigns

"Thus it seems that on the Second of July the two armies were departing as fast as the orders of the commanding generals and the legs of the soldiers could widen the space", (1) General Smith wrote this well after the war was over, but the spectacle of both armies retreating from the battlefield at Malvern Hill made an indelible impression on him, one that he would retain for the rest of his life.

Baldy Smith was so distraught over the failure of McClellan and the campaign that he applied for a leave of absence to go to Washington and ask for another assignment. In the end, he placed greater importance on his relationships with General Franklin, the Sixth Corps and his division and returned to duty with his troops. (2)

McClellan's relationship with Smith changed too. Without question, Smith's remarks about his actions had reached him and McClellan was intolerant of any criticism. He had cashiered one division commander, Brigadier General Charles Hamilton for sending criticisms to members of Congress. (3) On July 18, 1862, McClellan wrote to his wife about Smith, "Smith went off today. I don't think he intends returning . . . . he had not even the decency to bid me good bye after all I have done for him, ... I don't care to have him come back." (4)

In 1866, McClellan wrote about his former subordinates. "W.F. Smith was undoubtedly a man of high order of ability; he possessed great personal courage, and a wonderfully quick eye for ground and handling of troops. On the other hand he was indolent, not a good administrator, not well versed in the details of service. He was also too quick tempered towards those under him, very selfish, & had a most bitter tongue which often ran away with him and got him in trouble. Smith was one of those personalities who must always intrigue the acts of those above him. He did much harm in that way. His faults incapacitated him from ever being more than a comdr of a Corp. Probably there was no one under me who owed so much to me as he did, & from no one did I meet with such causeless ingratitude." These words were written for McClellan's autobiography but removed the literary executor. (5)

During his stay at Harrison's Landing, McClellan spent his time blaming the Lincoln Administration for his failure on the Peninsula and calling for more troops. President Lincoln visited the Union camp at Harrison's Landing on July 8. McClellan handed the president what would be known as "the Harrison's Landing Letter" in which he attempted to get his old job as general-in-chief back and he again put forth his own political objectives for winning the war. Lincoln thanked McClellan for the letter and pocketed it. (6). Lincoln's next move was to name Major General Henry Halleck General-in-Chief on July 23, 1862 (7) (8)

Henry W. Halleck graduated from West Point in 1839, third in his class. He was sent to France to study fortifications and wrote several papers on military matters. He also translated the monumental works of Jomini. After a period of service, he resigned, became a lawyer, and was a very successful one in California. He entered the Civil War as a major general based upon General Scott's recommendation. Given command of the forces in the West, he was undeservedly credited with the successes of his subordinates, Grant, Pope and Curtiss. (9)

Baldy Smith was not impressed with Halleck. He wrote in his "Autobiography", "As to General [Henry W.] Halleck and his advice and the part he played at that time [July, August 1862] and after as General-in Chief and military advisor, I will say everything was bad and mischievous. He always looked wise, but never acted so, and it was a most unfortunate thing for the country he did not stick to the law and prepare briefs in place of the [illegible] command." (10)

Before Halleck was brought East, Major General John Pope, was brought from the West and given command of the Army of Virginia (11) That army was made up of three corps, Sigel's First Corps (formerly the Mountain Department), Bank's Second Corps (formerly the Department of the Shenandoah and before that The Fifth Corps of the Army of the Potomac)., and McDowell's Third Corps (formerly the Department of the Rappahannock and before that the First Corps of the Army of the Potomac).(12) Pope's assignment was to protect Washington, assure the safety of the Shenandoah Valley, and draw off the enemy around Richmond. (13) With the forces given him, Pope was ill equipped to fulfill his mission.

Pope was arrogant and generally disliked. He issued a set of orders between July10 and July 23 which called for living off the land in Virginia, holding Virginia citizens responsible for repairing any damage to railroads, wagon roads, and telegraph lines. These orders also called for the arrest of disloyal citizens "within the operations of the army". In one order he said he came from the West where they saw "the backs of the enemy". The insult was aimed at McClellan but was a slap to every soldier in the East. (14) There is good reason to believe that these orders were approved by Lincoln and Stanton and may have been written by Stanton. They were consistent with Lincoln's objective to destroy the will of the people of the South. (15) When General Fitz Porter heard of these orders, he wrote," I regret to see that Major General Pope has not improved since his youth and has now written himself down as what the military world has long known, an ass." (16)

Lincoln's concern, after the failure on the peninsula was to protect Washington. On August 3 Halleck ordered McClellan to leave Harrison's Landing and send his troops to join Pope. McClellan stalled as long as he could; the Sixth Corps didn't start to move until August 14. (17) After some hard marching, the corps reached Newport News on August 21 and started loading transports on that date. The corps arrived in Alexandria on August 23. (18) Writing to his wife, McClellan was critical of Franklin's slowness but recognized that Franklin had been ill. He added," I ought also to make a great deal of allowance for Smith also on the same account" (19)

While the Army of the Potomac was moving to join Pope, Porter sent reports to Washington that included criticisms of Pope. These reached Lincoln who wired McClellan about his concern whether Porter would cooperate with Pope's Army of Virginia, as he had been directed to do. McClellan assured Lincoln that Porter would do his duty, but it was one more issue with McClellan and his protégé.

The Second Battle of Bull Run took place on August 29 and 30. Delays caused by conflicting orders and lack of artillery resulted in the Sixth Corps arriving at Centerville, eight miles in the rear of the battlefield, on August 30. While the entire Army of the Potomac was supposed to join Pope, only the Third Corps under Heintzelman, the Fifth Corps under Porter, and Taylor's Brigade from the Sixth Corps actually participated in the battle. (20) As Franklin's Corps marched past Centerville on August 30 heading to the battlefield, it was met by "an indiscriminate mass of men, and wagons all going pell-mell to the rear." (21) Franklin fell back to Centerville and formed a line in an attempt to stop and form the stragglers. (22) The Second Battle of Bull Run was over; it was another Union defeat.

Porter's conduct in the battle became an issue. Brigadier General S. B. Roberts, the Inspector General of the Army of the Virginia, and not Pope, filed charges against Fitz Porter for disobeying Pope's orders. A court-martial found Porter guilty and he was discharged from the army. Pope had lost track of the actual situation on the ground and had issued orders that could not be obeyed. Colonel Esposito, writing in the West Point Atlas of the Civil War said, "Twenty years later, when the real circumstances became known his [Porter's] sentence was remitted." (23)

General Smith met the charges against his classmate, Porter, with disbelief. He wrote in his Memoirs, "The day after the battle of Chantilly [September 2, 1862] the army remained at Fairfax C.H. There I remember seeing Porter and Pope evidently discussing future movements and seemingly on the very best of terms, and later on, when I read Pope's charges against Porter, I could but conclude that the charges were the outcome of some conferences taking place later at the War Dept. It is impossible that Pope could have thought at Fairfax C.H. that Porter had positively disobeyed orders." (24) Later, Smith would also be subjected to Stanton's campaign against McClellan and his associates

The circumstances surrounding Porter's court-martial and the his subsequent exoneration in 1878 suggest that Smith was probably right in believing the charges were likely "cooked up" in Washington. Both Porter and McClellan were relieved on November 7, 1862. The court martial against Porter started on November 25, 1862 based on charges made by Pope's inspector general. Stanton, who detested McClellan and any associated with him, appointed the officers of the court. Most of these officers received promotions after they delivered their verdict. (25)

Pope was finished in the East and shipped off to the Northwest Territory to deal with the Sioux Indians. Private William B.

Westervelt, 27th N.Y. Volunteers of the Sixth Corps put it succinctly," Pope blazed forth like a meteor and disappeared about as quick, and as complete" (26)

On September 2, Lincoln and Halleck went to McClellan's home in Washington and asked him to command the forces around Washington. (27)

CHAPTER 10

The Return of McClellan

General McClellan wrote his wife on August 24, 1862, "[if] Pope is beaten in which case they may want me to save Washington again." (1) Lincoln's appraised McClellan's actions in speaking to John Hay, "He [McClellan] had acted badly toward Pope; he really wanted him to fail" (2) With this backdrop, it is apparent that Lincoln's act in restoring McClellan was one of desperation. The simple fact was that "McClellan had the confidence of the army." (3) McClellan confided to his wife "I only consent to take it for my country's sake & with the humble hope that God has called me to it—now pray that he may support me! Don't be worried—my conscience is clear & I trust in God."(4)

While McClellan prayed for the support of God, he did not have the trust of Lincoln's cabinet. Lincoln liked to work with his cabinet and have the members support him. Lincoln announced his decision to the cabinet when he met with them a few hours after restoring McClellan to power. The cabinet was stunned. McClellan's superior, Secretary of War Stanton, had written and circulated a petition to have McClellan removed. He had obtained the signatures of Secretary of the Treasury Chase; Attorney General Bates, Postmaster General Blair, in addition to his own. Secretary of the Interior Smith was prepared to sign the petition, and Secretary of the Navy Wells agreed in principle. According to Gideon Welles "Lincoln acknowledged that General McClellan suffered from the "slows" and was "good for nothing" in an offensive campaign. But in the present situation, with the need to defend Washington and reorganize the beaten troops and restore their morale, there was no one better." Still, General McClellan was in a very tenuous situation (5)

Baldy Smith's reaction to McClellan's restoration to command was mildly positive. He said," I felt that the leader better than McClellan had not yet appeared." (6) This was damning the general with faint praise.

On September 3 Lincoln sent an order to Halleck "to organize an army for active operations, from all the material within and coming within his control, independent of the forces necessary for the defense of Washington, when such active army shall take the field." (7) General Halleck avoided accepting responsibility and immediately turned the task over to McClellan. (8)

With remarkable speed, McClellan organized the "New" Army of the Potomac. Uncertain about the location of Lee's army, the Young Napoleon advanced with his army spread over a front of more than 30 miles as it headed for Frederick, Maryland. Smith's division, a part of the Sixth Corps, was on the extreme left, near the Potomac River. It departed from the Washington area on September 6. (9)

One week later, September 13, 1862, Union soldiers near Frederick found a copy of Lee's Special Order 191, which became known as "the Lost Order." The order sent Generals Jackson, McLaws, and Walker (West Point 1850) to capture the garrison at Harper's Ferry and remove the threat to Lee's supply line; Longstreet was sent to Boonsboro; and D. H. Hill was made the army's rear guard and was to follow the main army to Boonsboro. (10) General McClellan wired General Halleck at 11:00 P.M. on September 13t that the order had "come into my hands this evening." (11) McClellan then sent orders to General Franklin that night directing him to march at daybreak on the morning of September 14 "by Jefferson and Burkittsville upon the road to Rohersville." He continued, "I have reliable information that the mountain pass [Crampton's Pass] by this road is practicable for artillery and wagons" (12)

Franklin's orders were "to cut off, destroy, or capture McLaws command and relieve Colonel Miles (West Point 1824) [and the garrison at Harper's Ferry]." Franklin was further told that if he found the pass held by a large force of the enemy, he was to start his attack "about half an hour after you hear severe fighting at the pass [Turner's Gap] on the Hagerstown pike where the main body will attack." (13)

Smith's division reached Burkittsville around 1:00 P.M. on September 14. The little village is at the foot of the eastern side of South Mountain and Crampton's Pass is a road through a narrow defile at the summit. The climb on the east side of the mountain is particularly steep and pushing a corps through that narrow gap was akin to pouring a large quantity of liquid through a very small funnel. The mountain was covered with growth making it difficult to locate the enemy. The Confederates had good artillery and they had stone walls for cover. A small force could easily defend the pass.

General Howell Cobb was in charge of the Confederate forces on the mountain. He said that his forces there did not exceed 2,200 men. (14) Franklin's corps had a strength of 12,300. (15) Despite the numerical difference, the Rebels had the advantage of terrain, stone walls and artillery.

Slocum's division was on the right of the Union line and opened the battle around 3:00 P.M. (16) Colonel Joseph Bartlett had the lead brigade and the 27th N.Y. was in that unit. The 27th's historian wrote "On went our line, up the side of the steep mountain, so steep in many places that the men had to pull themselves up by taking hold of the bushes" (17)

After Slocum's attack began, General Franklin ordered Smith to attack. He was to turn the enemy's right flank. The Union attack was successful and the Confederates were driven off the mountain and into Pleasant Valley. The battle ended after dark, it was too late to pursue the retreating Rebels. (18) The Sixth Corps lost 533. (19) The Confederate loss was around 800 plus 400 prisoners. (20)

General Longstreet summed up the battle, "The Confederates made a bold effort to hold, but the attack was too well organized and too cleverly pushed to leave the matter long in doubt. Their flanks being severely crowded upon soon began to drop off, when a sweeping charge of Slocum's line gained the position. The brigades of General Brooks (West Point 1841) and Colonel Irwin of Smith's division were advanced to Slocum's left and joined in the pursuit, which was so rapid that the Confederates were not able to rally a good line, and the entire mountain was abandoned to the Federals and the pursuit ended." (21)

Union forces at Turner's Gap had been equally successful. Around 8:00 P.M. on September 14, Lee wired McLaws, "the day has gone against us, and the army will go by way of Sharpsburg and cross the river." (22) At 8:00 A.M. on September 15, McClellan wired General Halleck that he was sure that he had achieved a great victory, and had learned that "the enemy is making for Shepherdstown in a perfect panic, and General Lee had last night stated publicly that he must admit they had been shockingly whipped." (23)

This picture changed rapidly. At 8:15 P.M. on September 14, Jackson sent this message to Lee, ". . . I look to Him [God] for complete success tomorrow." (24)

After the Confederates were driven off the mountain, General McLaws assembled a force to repel the expected Sixth Corps attack. He "formed [a] line of battle across the valley about one and one-half miles below Crampton's Gap with the remnants of General Cobb's, Semmes', and Mahone's brigades and those of Wilcox (West Point 1846), Kershaw, and Barksdale." (25)

The strength of McLaws' division on September 15, when it faced Franklin in Pleasant Valley, is hard to nail down. However, Confederate reports indicate that McLaws had 8,000 on that date, a figure that seems reasonable. (26) His returns for September 30 show an even greater strength of 12,112 (27)

General Franklin rode from the eastern side of the mountain over the crest at 7:00 A.M. on September 15. He had an excellent view of the Pleasant Valley below and could see the Confederate line of battle. Any attack would have to been made by Smith's division of 4500; Slocum's men were worn out from fighting the day before. Franklin and Smith conferred at the western base of South Mountain but the attack was overtaken by events. The commander at Harper's Ferry, Colonel Dixon Miles, ordered that the white flag of surrender go up at 7:30 A.M. and all fighting stopped an hour later. (28)

McClellan then ordered Franklin "to remain where he was, to watch the large force in front of him and to protect our left and rear until the night of the 16th when he was ordered to join the main body of the army at Keedysville, after sending Brigadier General Darius Couch (West Point 1846) and his division to Maryland Heights." (29)

CHAPTER 11

Antietam and the End of McClellan

Smith and his division left their camp near Crampton's Pass at 6:00 A.M. on September 17, and arrived at the battlefield at Antietam around 10:00 A. M. (1) He reported to General McClellan at his headquarters and was told to hold his division on the road to Sharpsburg ready to support an attack on the right or the left, as needed, (2) (3) Shortly after that, Smith was ordered to join General Sumner on the right of the Union line. Fording Antietam Creek, Smith reached his designated position and sent his regiments to aid the Union batteries that were unsupported. (4)

Confederates infantry advanced toward the threatened batteries and Smith sent Colonel Irwin and his brigade to stop them. Irwin's brigade did so and then remained in place. The brigade's position was near the Dunkard Church where it was subjected to intensive artillery fire from the West Woods. (5)

. General Franklin arrived on the field after Smith did, and found General Sumner in a depressed state of mind. The First Corps and the Twelfth Corps had lost their leaders, Hooker and Mansfield (West Point 1822), and had been fought out. Sedgwick (West Point 1837) and his division of the Second Corps had suffered severe losses in the West Woods. Franklin organized his Sixth Corps for an attack but Sumner, the senior officer on that part of the field, forbade it. McClellan came on the field and when Franklin appealed to him, he upheld Sumner. The Sixth Corps, ready to fight, was denied the opportunity to do so. (6)

Later in the day McClellan came to Franklin's headquarters and Franklin proposed taking a hill (Nicodemus Hill) on the Confederate left in the morning of September 18. The attack was to have been made by the entire Sixth Corps and if successful would have commanded the West Woods. (7) General McClellan agreed to the proposal and then, during the night, countermanded it. The reason he gave was that he expected 18,000 additional troops to arrive on September 18, and when they did he would renew the order. (8)

General Smith was incensed that during the battle, General Sumner had given direct orders to two of his brigades without his knowledge. The first was to Colonel Irwin, the second to General William Brooks (West Point 1841). When Smith learned that Brooks had been sent to relieve General Israel Richardson's (West Point 1841) division, he countermanded the order and placed Brooks in a gap between his own division and Richardson's. (9)

General Richardson was mortally wounded by Confederate artillery fire around 1:00 P.M. (10) Smith's best brigade commander, General Winfield Scott Hancock, was immediately assigned to command the First Division of Sumner's Second Corps. (11)

On the Union left, Burnside and the Ninth Corps were at the lower bridge over the Antietam (later called Burnside Bridge). Prior to the battle McClellan had reassigned Hooker and his First Corps from Burnside's wing command to a corps reporting directly to himself. This left Burnside with only the Ninth Corps. Burnside refused to accept the change as other than temporary and continued to act as a wing commander. When, at 10:00 A.M., McClellan ordered Burnside to attack, he simply passed the order to General Cox who was given command of the Ninth Corps at the Battle of Antietam. (12) Cox was a political general with no previous military training or experience before the war, (13) He understood that his orders were "to create a diversion in favor of the main attack", as McClellan stated in his preliminary report on the battle.(14) That was what he attempted to do.

Cox's men did not find a way to cross the Antietam Creek until about 3:00 P.M. and did not move forward toward the village of Sharpsburg until then. By that time Confederate General A. P. Hill appeared on the field, after the capture of Harper's Ferry, with his men dressed in Federal uniforms. Hill stopped the Federal offensive on the left and the battle was over.

In his autobiography, General Smith criticized General Cox: "General O.B. Wilcox (West Point 1847) and [Colonel] Scammon

(West Point 1837) 'had formed an assaulting party which would have done the needful work before [General Ambrose P.] Hill arrived from Harper's Ferry. General Cox declined to allow them to make the assault. They appealed to General Burnside who, without going to inform himself of the situation, ordered them to do as General Cox directed. . . . . Had there been anything of Napoleon in McClellan, Burnside would have been relieved, before nine o'clock [a.m.] on the 17ᵗʰ of September, 1862, by a fighting general. Lee's right flank would have been crushed . . ." (15)

September 18 the day after the great battle, the two armies remained in place, but did not fight. The night of the 18 Smith said, "I slept on the ground in the mud with a rail for my pillow. . . . . I heard the first wheel as it turned when Lee began to fall back. I jumped to my feet but concluding that everything would be known at headquarters, I returned to my bed . . . ." (16) Later in the day Smith said "On entering headquarters we received the news that *Lee had retreated across the Potomac*". (17)

President Lincoln felt that McClellan had an opportunity to destroy Lee's army and, instead, let it escape. He never forgave McClellan. (18) The Army of the Potomac remained in the Sharpsburg area until September 26 with the Sixth Corps crossing the Potomac the first days of November. (19) Initially, McClellan has no intention of moving and no plans when he did move. (20) (21)

Early in October, General Smith was summoned to McClellan's headquarters. McClellan handed him a draft of a letter to President Lincoln about the preliminary Emancipation Proclamation that the president had issued on September 22. The draft conveyed the idea that the army had not enlisted to put down slavery which was preserved by the Constitution. It strongly dissented to the terms of the proclamation. Smith begged McClellan not to send the letter for he felt that it would destroy McClellan. He remembered that the letter was discarded in his presence.

Mark Snell, in *From First to Last, The Life of Major General William B. Franklin*, writes: "McClellan, Franklin, Porter, Smith, and many of the other generals holding divisional and brigade commands were politically conservative. In their minds and hearts, the only reason to prosecute the war was to end the rebellion and reunite the country to way it was before the conflict." (22)

Smith was surprised to read McClellan's General Orders No, 123 which the Young Napoleon issued to the troops with a copy to the president. The order called upon the army to support the administration. Then he added this key sentence "The remedy for political errors, if any are committed, is to be found only in the action of the people at the polls". (23) (24) When Smith saw the order he was both surprised and annoyed. Smith felt the order portrayed a state of dissatisfaction within the army that didn't exist. (25)

On November 7 President Lincoln relieved McClellan and replaced him with General A. P. Burnside. Smith offered his opinion about the change. "If there was at any time after the Battle of Antietam any propriety in relieving McClellan from the command it should have been done before the army crossed into Virginia." (26) Smith's appraisal of Burnside was that he was cautious and not a strong man. "The result was we knew nothing of him—of opinions he had none save the reflections of the last person with whom he talked. With all this there was the intense stubbornness which sometimes takes hold of weak minds, and then *sauve qui peut. (Every man for himself)*." (27) Smith also said—presumably at the time of Burnside's appointment—"General Franklin should have commanded the army, and would have done so, if he had not erroneously been supposed to be the devoted adherent of General McClellan". (28)

CHAPTER 12

Fredericksburg—Burnside's Plans
November 7-December 12, 1862

The mid-term elections held on November 4 went against the Administration, "with a Democratic swing that was only one step removed from a disaster" wrote Historian Fletcher Pratt. (1) Lincoln felt that something had to be done. Burnside was a member of the War Democrats whose support Lincoln needed and he was the only senior officer in the East to have had a successful campaign—his expedition on the North Carolina Coast. (2) Hence, his appointment was based on both political and military considerations

In addition to replacing McClellan, President Lincoln replaced Don Carlos Buell (West Point 1841) with William Rosecrans in the Tennessee-Kentucky theatre, and Benjamin F. Butler with Nathaniel Banks with headquarters in New Orleans. Halleck's biographer Marsalek said" The new commanders knew what was expected of them; forward movement." (3)

Ambrose Burnside was convinced that he was not up to the job. In testimony before the Joint Committee on the Conduct of the War on December 19, 1862, Burnside pointed out that he had declined twice to accept the offer to command the army, which he felt he was not competent to command it, and that he mulled over Lincoln's last offer with his staff officers and General McClellan. The officers and McClellan told him "that this was an order which I, as a soldier, had to obey." (4)

General Burnside's actions during the period when he was commander of the Army of the Potomac followed General Smith's appraisal precisely. He had difficulty making decisions, often contradicted himself, stubbornly stuck to a decision once made, and would accept responsibility for failure at first and then later blame others, particularly those who thought they were his friends.

One of General Burnside's first actions was to reorganize the Army of the Potomac. On November 16 he formed the army into three grand divisions. The Right Grand Division was led by General Sumner, with the Second Corps under Couch, and the Ninth under Wilcox; the Center Grand Division was led by Hooker, with the Third Corps under Stoneman and the Fifth Corps under Butterfield; the Left Grand Division was led by Franklin, with the First Corps under Reynolds and the Sixth Corps under Smith. (5)

Thus, on November 16, 1862, Baldy Smith was given corps command for the first time He was promoted to major general; with his new rank making him eligible for that post. His promotion was subject to Senate approval and that action was not taken before the Battle of Fredericksburg.

General Burnside hastened to develop a plan for the coming campaign. He "fretted himself to long hours of work, went almost without sleep, and became physically ill."(6) Appointed to command the Army of the Potomac on November 7 Burnside submitted his plan for the campaign just two days later, November 9. (7) Halleck and Burnside met on November 12 to discuss it. They disagreed, but President Lincoln approved Burnside's plan on November 14. In the process Burnside agreed to amend his plan so that he would get to Fredericksburg by way of the fords above that city. General Halleck in his report and Historians T. Williams and W.A. Craft indicate that Burnside did not make the changes he had agreed to. Instead, he marched to the north side of the Rappahannock and required pontoons to build bridges to cross it. (8) (9) The pontoons did not arrive until November 25. (10) (11)

The wait for the pontoons gave the Confederates time to assemble on the hills around Fredericksburg, get their artillery in place and build defenses. Longstreet reached Fredericksburg on November 19 and Jackson reached there around the end of November. (12)

In a letter dated November 24 to his friend, Carl Schurz, Lincoln complained that Burnside was not moving fast enough. The general had been in command 17 days! The president then traveled to Burnside's headquarters on November 26 and had Burnside come to Washington and confer with him and Halleck on the November 27. (13) (14) In that meeting, Lincoln put forth his own plan for the campaign. It was a complicated one and both Halleck and Burnside ruled it out on the basis that it would take too long to implement. (15) By rejecting the president's plan, Burnside created more pressure on himself for he had to come up with his own plan.

Early in December, Burnside called a council of war to explain his plan of attack at Skinker's Neck which was about twelve miles below Fredericksburg on the Rappahannock. All but Hooker approved of it. Shortly after that council, Smith visited headquarters and learned that Burnside had changed his mind; the army would cross at Fredericksburg. Smith's comment to Burnside was that "you can force a passage here at any point, which I do not doubt—but what are you going to do with those hills . . . . It strikes me your serious work will only begin when you get on the other bank." Burnside's response was that he expected to surprise Lee, (16)

General Burnside had 113, 000 men present for duty on November 10 and 147 guns. (17) Lee had 78,228 men (18) and 306 guns. (19) Lee was able to fortify the heights at Fredericksburg and create defenses for troops and artillery that were nearly impregnable. General Andrew A. Humphrey (West Point 1831) pointed out that in the Civil War "the strength of an army sustaining attack was more than quadrupled." (20) Using this figure, the strength of the Confederates at Fredericksburg would have been equal to 312,912 men or an advantage of 2.7 to 1. The ratio of Confederate artillery to that of Union artillery was slightly more than 2 to 1. Further, the Confederate artillery was well protected and most of the Union artillery was out of range.

Smith's command crossed the river on December 11 and 12. After examining the terrain, Smith and Franklin concluded that an attack in force should be made from their left front. On the December 12 Burnside came to Franklin's headquarters. and in a meeting that lasted an hour, Franklin and Smith presented their plan. General Burnside responded enthusiastically with "Yes, Yes." (21)

General Smith stated ". . . when he left we told him what we had to do and begged that the orders might be sent at once to which he most positively assented. The plan of battle proposed to him was this, viz. the 6th Corps was to be drawn out of its line after dark and formed in column of attack to sleep on its arms and be ready for action at daylight. It was to be relieved in its position by the 3rd Corps while the 1[St] Corps was to be held in reserve for use either with the 3rd or 6th as required. The attack was to be made in the direction of the Old Stage Road to Richmond with a view of turning Lee's right flank. The effective force of the Sixth Corps was about 25,000 men and of the First Corps about 15,000 (22)

After General Burnside left Franklin's headquarters, Franklin, Smith and Reynolds remained up, dressed and ready for action. All of the planning and movement of troops had been made according to the plan Franklin and Smith had put forward. But General Burnside did not go to his headquarters and write out the orders then. Instead, he said in his report," <u>By the night of the 12, the troops were all in position and I visited the different commands with a view as to determine future movements</u>." (Underlining supplied) (23) At that late stage before the battle, it appears General Burnside had not settled on any plan.

CHAPTER 13

The Battle of Fredericksburg
December 13, 1862

Brigadier General James Hardie of Burnside's staff delivered the Commanding General's orders. The written orders arrived around 8:00 A.M. (1) The orders were dated 5:55 A.M. and were scribbled in pencil. Hardie had stopped for an hour and a half for breakfast before delivering them. (2)

General Hardie was no ordinary aide; his role at Fredericksburg encompassed reporting, evaluating and defending Franklin's actions and being a part of the Left Grand Division's leadership. It was an amazing variety of roles for one individual.

Hardie's father was a wealthy New York State real estate broker and a political and personal friend of President Martin Van Buren. (3) It was the president who appointed young Hardie to West Point in 1839 at the age if sixteen. He graduated in the same class as Franklin, where Franklin was #1 and he was #11 in the Class of 1843. (4)

In September, 1861 Hardie was assigned to McClellan's staff as a lieutenant colonel. When Burnside assumed command of the Army of the Potomac, he recommended Hardie for promotion to brigadier general. The recommendation was supported by Generals Grant, Hooker, Wool, Hancock, Reynolds, Franklin, Humphreys, and Butterfield. (5) He was commissioned as a brigadier general on November 29, 1862. (6)

Burnside sent General Hardie to be with the Left Grand Division during the attack. He did not send anyone to be with the other Grand Divisions on December 13, 1862. Excerpts from the order from Burnside follow. "General Hardie will carry this dispatch to you, and remain with you during the day. The general commanding directs that you keep your whole command in position for a rapid movement down the old Richmond road, and you will send out at once a division at least to pass below Smithfield, to seize, if possible, the height near Captain Hamilton's on this side of the Massaponax taking care to keep it well supported and its line of retreat open. He has ordered another column of a division or more to be moved from General Sumner's command up the Plank road to its intersection with the Telegraph road, where they will divide, with a view to seizing the heights on both of these roads. Holding these two heights, with the heights near Captain Hamilton's will, he hopes, compel the enemy to evacuate the whole ridge between these points . . . . You will keep your command in readiness to move at once as soon as the fog lifts . . . ." (7)

On the night of December 12 when General Burnside heard the plan that Franklin and Smith proposed he exclaimed "Yes, Yes" and agreed to send confirming orders promptly.(8) Smith and Franklin had every reason to believe that the orders received were what they expected. General Smith was at Franklin's headquarters when Burnside's order arrived. He indicated that Franklin had "made all the arrangements in his power for the execution for the order based upon the supposition that the order would be for an attack in force . . . . General Franklin showed the order immediately to Genl. Reynolds and myself and the conclusion of all of us was that Genl. Burnside determined not to adopt the plan of making the attack in force from the left. . . . . No one differed on what was intended by the order and that was to send a division well supported and immediately report its [the orders] receipt. (9)

General Franklin testified before the Joint Committee on the Conduct of the War, on March 28, 1863, "I consulted with my corps commanders [Smith and Reynolds] about this order as it was not what we expected and concluded that it meant that there should be what is termed as an armed reconnaissance, or observation in force made of the enemy's lines, with one division; that in order that that division might not be utterly destroyed I was to keep it well supported, but the main point of the order, twice referred to, was that the command should be kept in readiness for a rapid movement along the Richmond road."(10) In that same testimony, General Franklin stated," But I did not suppose that this order involved the main attack. I was supported in this opinion by the staff officer [General Hardie] who brought the order." (11)

The difficulties of understanding what Burnside intended are illustrated by the comments of the experts. General Palfrey, writing in the *Campaigns of the Civil War* on Fredericksburg in 1882, "This order is exceedingly hard to understand, even at this distance of time, and with all the light that has been thrown on it." "The fault was in the orders and not in any failure on Franklin's part to understand them and obey them." (12) Colonel Esposito, in the *West Point Atlas of the Civil War*, wrote," Unfortunately, his [Burnsides'] written orders for the 13 were vague. Franklin was to send a division to seize the high ground near Hamilton's; Sumner was to push up the Telegraph road, both were to be ready to advance their commands. It was hoped, optimistically, that those two weak attacks would force the Confederates to evacuate the whole ridge. This order makes sense only if Burnside still believed that only a part of Lee's army was confronting him." (13)

The assignment to send out a division was given to General Reynolds and his First Corps. That corps was on the extreme left of the Federal line. The division to lead the attack was Meade's, supported by the divisions of Gibbon on the left and Doubleday on the right.

As soon as Meade was in motion, a strong force of the enemy assaulted the extreme left. It was in a position where it could fire into Meade's rear as he advanced. Reynolds halted Meade's attack until the enemy could be driven off. Then Meade advanced and reached the crest of the hill when additional Rebel troops arrived and drove him back. The fighting was fierce and continued until after 2:30 P.M., when Gibbon was wounded. (14) By 3:40 P.M., Hardie reported to Burnside that "Gibbon's and Meade's divisions are badly used up, and I fear another attack on the enemy on our left cannot be made this afternoon." (15)

From 7:30 A.M. to 4:30 P.M. on that fateful December 13, General Hardie sent fifteen telegrams to General Burnside. To understand General Franklin's actions during the battle, it is important to look at Hardie's role for he was Burnside's alter-ego on the scene.

In Hardie's first message to Burnside dated 9:15 A.M. on December 12 he asks for more artillery for Franklin. Here Hardie acted as staff to Franklin. (16)

His sixth telegram to Burnside dated December 13 at 12:45 P.M. was that "General Meade's line is advancing in the direction you prescribed this morning." Here Hardie is reporting. (17)

His fifteenth and last telegram to Burnside was at 4:30 P.M. ". . . . A new attack has been opened on our left: but the left is safe, though it is too late to advance, either to the left or the front." Again, Hardie is acting as a member of Franklin's staff. (18)

During the course of the battle, General Burnside sent three aides de camp to General Franklin. The first, Captain P.M. Lydig, went to Franklin's headquarters and returned around 12:30 P.M. He reported that Meade was "very hotly engaged" and that none of Smith's Sixth Corps were involved the attack. The second aide de camp, Captain J. M. Cutts, delivered an order to Franklin around 2:00 P.M. "to advance his right and front." Franklin told Cutts that it was impossible to advance. The third aide de camp, Captain R.H. Goddard, delivered Burnside's last order around 3:00 P.M. That order was, "tell General Franklin, with my compliments, that I wish him to make a vigorous attack with his whole force, 'our right is hard pressed' (19) Hardie was present with Franklin when the order was received. Goddard reported, "Either General Franklin or General Hardie told me all the forces were engaged except Burn's division which was guarding the bridges." In his report, Burnside said, "this order was not carried out." (20)

When General Hooker was ordered to advance, he said it was to "attack the enemy on the telegraph road—the same position we had been butting against all day long." Upon receiving the order he sent an aide to General Burnside advising him that the attack should not be made at that place. The aide returned indicating that Burnside said the attack must be made. Hooker then went in person to Burnside to appeal Burnside's decision, but Burnside insisted that his order be carried out and it was, resulting in more casualties. (21)

General Sumner attacked as ordered and said "the attack failed owing to the enemy's fortifications being much more formidable that we had supposed them to be." (22) If Sumner's and Burnside's decisions were as Sumner claimed, the attempt to feel out the enemy turned into a disastrous battle. Once engaged Burnside stubbornly refused to listen to two of his senior generals, Franklin and Hooker, and intensified the fighting.

The Federal losses at Fredericksburg were as follows:

	Killed	Wounded	Missing or Captured	Total
Franklin's Left Grand Division	373	2,697	653	3,723
Hooker's Center Grand Division	316	2,398	755	3,469
Sumner's Right Grand Division	491	3,993	737	5,161
Total	1,180	9,028	2,145	12,353

Most of Franklin's losses were in Meade's division. Meade went into the fight with 4,500 men and lost 40% of them.

The major issue at Fredericksburg was whether Meade's attack would have been successful if he had been supported. General Lee wrote, "The attack on the 13 had been so easily repulsed and by so small a part of our army, that it was not supposed the enemy would limit his efforts to an attempt which . . . . seemed comparatively insignificant." (23)

General Smith wrote, on February 4, 1863, ". . . . I have seen a map sent to me by General Butterfield made by the topographical officer of the Rebel General Jackson's command giving the position of Jackson's troops opposite our line. Since seeing that I am fully of the opinion that the only possible chance of our success on that day lay in making such an attack as I have indicated and at least with the force indicated [against the Confederate right with 40,000 men]." (24)

CHAPTER 14

Fredericksburg—Aftermath
December 14, 1862-May 31, 1863

Events moved rapidly in this period and were important in understanding their impact upon General Smith.

December 17, 1862—Initially, Burnside accepted the blame for the failure at Fredericksburg. He wrote, in his report of December 17 to General Halleck, "For the failure in the attacks I am responsible, as the extreme gallantry, courage, and endurance shown by them [the brave officers and men] was never excelled and would have carried the points, had it been possible." (1)

December 18, 1862—General Burnside met with General Halleck and Secretary Stanton at Aquia Landing. (2) There is no record of this meeting in the Official Records.

December 19, 1862—The Joint Committee on the Conduct of the War (Hereafter referred to as the Joint Committee) met in Washington where General Burnside testified before them. When asked about the conduct of the officers and men at the Battle of Fredericksburg, he stated, "With the exception of a single regiment, it was excellent" He continued, "Every man was put in column of attack that could be got in."(3)

General Franklin also testified before the Joint Committee on this date. He said, 'It's my opinion that if, instead of making two real attacks, our whole force had been concentrated on our left—that is, our available force—and the real attack had been made there, and merely a feint made upon the right, we might have carried the heights." (4)

December 20, 1862—General Hooker testified before the Joint Committee on this date. He said he had advocated "keeping the army together and turning the enemy's right. I did not approve the attempt to pierce so strong a line at two points, when one would be as much as we would be likely to succeed in."(5) Hooker added, gratuitously, "I do not know the facts, but I have understood that a large portion of Franklin's force was not engaged at all." (6)

General Sumner testified before the Joint Committee He was asked whether it was possible to carry the heights. His response was "that if, instead of making two real attacks, our whole force had been concentrated on the; left—that is, our available force—and the real attack had been made there, and merely a feint made upon the right, we might have carried the heights."(7) Hooker's and Sumner's positions are significant for they are the same as that proposed by Franklin and Smith on the eve of the battle; one which Burnside initially accepted and then rejected.

On this date, also, Franklin and Smith addressed a letter to President Lincoln. While this appears to be unusual, Franklin had participated in meetings with the president in early 1862 and Lincoln had depended upon his generals, including Franklin, in reorganizing the army into a corps structure and in approving the plans for the Peninsular Campaign. (8) Given this background, Franklin apparently felt free to suggest a different strategy for the Army of the Potomac. Franklin and Smith devoted their letter to plans; there was no reference, direct or indirect, to General Burnside."(9)

In their letter Franklin and Smith proposed amassing all the troops available in the East on both sides of the James River, supported by the Navy, and attacking and capturing Richmond. The problem with the proposal was that it did not meet two of Lincoln's main objectives i.e. destroying Lee's army and protecting Washington. (10) Lincoln simply sent the letter to his military advisors.

James Harrison Wilson later wrote: "The letter was doubtless written in entire good faith, but at a time when it seemed to be impossible for the government, even if it had so desired, to carry out its recommendations. Its only immediate effect was to arouse the antagonism of Mr. Stanton against these two able officers, and to deprive the country for a while of their services. A wiser and more temperate Secretary of War would have filed and ignored it, or sent for the officers and explained why he deemed their advice to be impracticable at that time. That, however, was not Mr. Stanton's way. Although intensely patriotic and in earnest, he was imperious and overbearing both in high and low alike, and preferred to banish and offend rather than listen and conciliate." (11)

December 26, 1862—On the 26 of December, Burnside ordered the troops to prepare to attack at a sight seven miles below Fredericksburg at a point opposite the Sedden House. (12) Brigadier General Newton, commander of the Third Division of the Sixth Corps, a career engineer, looked at the proposed place of crossing the river, and was convinced that the plan was faulty and would lead to another disaster. He was granted leave by General Smith to go to Washington where he planned to voice his concerns to a member of the Joint Committee on the Conduct of the War.

Newton took Brigadier General Cochrane, commander of the First Brigade in Newton's division and a political general, with him. Unable to find any member of the committee, Cochrane arranged a meeting with President Lincoln on January 30. Newton's concerns were (1) that Burnside had selected a place to cross that was "as bad, if not a little worse, than the place we had crossed at the first time" and (2) the troops were dissatisfied with Burnside's military capacity" (13) Lincoln was alarmed at Newton's report and he was surprised that Burnside planned an attack without his approval

After Newton left the president's office, Lincoln sent this message to General Burnside, "December 30, 1862, 3:30 P.M I have good reason for saying you must not make a general movement of the army without letting me know." (14)

Upon receiving the president's order, General Burnside went to Washington to meet with Lincoln. The president told him that "two general officers of his command had informed him of the proposed movement, that if carried out would result in disaster" The president refused to name the officers. Secretary Stanton and General Halleck joined the meeting

Later, in conversations with his generals at his headquarters, General Burnside stated positively that he told the president that he should resign and the officers and soldiers in the army had no confidence in Stanton and Halleck and that they should be replaced. He did this in the presence of Halleck and Stanton. He put these views in a letter to the president dated January 1, 1863. (15)

In a letter to President Lincoln dated January 5, 1863, Burnside wrote, "In conversation with you on New Year's morning, I was led to express some opinions which I afterwards felt it my duty to place on paper, and to express them verbally to the gentlemen of whom we were speaking, which I did in your presence after handing you the letter. You were not disposed then, as I saw, to retain the letter and I took it back, but I now return it to you for record, if you wish it." (16)

Burnside's letter to the president dated January 1, 1863, repeats his position that Halleck and Stanton should be removed. The footnote in the Official Records indicates the letter was "published from General Burnside's copy; it does not appear among Mr. Lincoln's papers." (17)

January 20, 1863—The army started to move north of Falmouth on January 20 the intent was to cross the Rappahannock River near Banks Ford. Burnside planned to cross on bridges built with pontoons. Heavy rains ensued, and the ground, which had been frozen, turned to mud. At 7:30 A.M on January 20. Smith sent a message to Franklin saying," It is not possible to get these boats into the river so that we can make a fight today; and the enemy will have all night to concentrate against us. (18) By January 22 the "Mud March" ended and the troops returned to their quarters (19) It was another Union failure.

January 23, 1863—General Burnside learned the names of the officers who met with Lincoln. He prepared his General Orders No. 8 in which he proposed to dismiss Generals Hooker, Brooks, Newton, and Cochrane from the army. He also proposed to relieve from duty with the Army of the Potomac, Generals Franklin, Smith, Sturgis (West Point 1846), Ferraro and Lieutenant Colonel Taylor. (20) After preparing this order, he went to Washington and met with President Lincoln where he gave Lincoln a choice—approve the order or accept his resignation. The president then relieved Burnside from his position as commander of the Army of the Potomac but would not let him resign from the army. Lincoln then appointed Hooker as head of the Army of the Potomac, and relieved Sumner and Franklin from duty with that army. (21).

February 5, 1863—Baldy Smith was assigned to command the Ninth Corps and was transferred to Newport News, Virginia, (22) (23)

February 6, 1863—General Meade wrote a letter to his wife in which he said, "Baldy Smith has been relieved of his command and Sedgwick takes his corps [the Sixth Corps]—cause unknown, but supposed to be his affiliation with Franklin, and the fear that he would not cooperate with Hooker." (24)

February 7, 1863—General Burnside was called to testify before the Joint Committee on his administration of the Army of the Potomac from December 13, 1862 to January 20, 1863. In his testimony he criticized both Franklin and Hooker for their actions in the Battle of Fredericksburg. He also said that Newton and Cochrane should be dismissed from the army. (25)

February 9, 1863—General Newton appeared before the Joint Committee in Washington. The Committee tried to establish the point that Newton's visit with the president was initiated or approved by Franklin and Smith. Newton steadfastly insisted that he acted on his own. (26)

General Cochrane also appeared before the Joint Committee on this date. Again, members of the Joint Committee tried to get Cochrane to say that Franklin and Smith knew of or approved the reasons for his visit to Washington which resulted in meeting with the president. Cochrane said they did not. (27)

March 5, 1863—The Senate did not confirm Baldy Smith's appointment as major general. He was taken off the active duty list and was relieved from the command of the Ninth Corps. Smith then went to New York to await an assignment. (28)

<u>March 17, 1863</u>—General Meade wrote his wife, "My conversations with Burnside and Wade [Chairman of the Joint Committee] satisfied me that Franklin was to be made responsible for the failure at Fredericksburg and the Committee is seeking all the testimony they can procure to substantiate this theory of theirs." (29)

General Hardie was never called to appear before the Joint Committee. He was in a better position than anyone except Franklin to report on Burnside's orders and Franklin's actions.

<u>April 6, 1863</u>—The Joint Committee issued its report on Fredericksburg. The Committee wrote, "The testimony of all the witnesses before your committee proves most certainly that, had the attack been made from the left with all the force which General Franklin could have used for that purpose, the plan of General Burnside would have been completely successful, and our army would have achieved a most brilliant victory." (30)

The report was a document with a political agenda. It was released to the press before it was given to Congress, which had retired on March 4. It blamed Franklin for the failure at Fredericksburg. It failed to "discuss the bloodletting on the Union right" where Hooker, now head of the Army of the Potomac, was involved. Lastly, the report intimated that Franklin and Smith put Newton and Cochrane up to the talk with President Lincoln.

<u>First Week in May, 1863</u>—Franklin completed and distributed one thousand copies of a pamphlet titled, "A Reply of Maj. Gen. William B. Franklin, to the Report of the Joint Committee on the Conduct of the War, Submitted to the Public on the 6th of April, 1863." Franklin challenged every conclusion the Committee had reached. The pamphlet was sent to congressmen, cabinet members, newspaper editors and other men of influence. Baldy Smith, in New York, was a major distributor of the pamphlet. (31)

CHAPTER 15

The Gettysburg Campaign
June 10-July 15, 1863

General Hooker replaced General Burnside as commander of the Army of the Potomac on January 26, 1863. On February 5 Smith was assigned to command the Ninth Corps. Then, on March 9, 1863, General Smith and the Ninth Corps were transferred from the Army of the Potomac to Newport News, Virginia. (1)

Smith "parted from the 6th Corp with intense regret. "Battles and marches had made us intimate, and when a deputation followed me to the train it was with a heart too full for utterance that I said farewell. The grand old Army of the Potomac—the stay of the country in many a dark hour—its bravery, and patriotism was not dulled by mismanagement. It is my focal pride that I served with it and that my name will ever be on its records." Smith wrote in his autobiography "I had commanded one brigade of the 6th Corp from its formation, one division from its organization, and the 6th Corps after Burnside fell in command of the Army of the Potomac." (2)

In March Burnside was assigned command the Ninth Corps, his old corps. Smith was relieved and sent to New York to await another assignment

Referring to the Fredericksburg Campaign, Smith wrote, ". . . . I have always felt much responsibility for certain portions of the campaign, and in many respects my position was full of complications. Hooker caused me to be promptly relieved from duty with the army, which was progress for I had far less confidence in him than in Burnside. I was also followed by the Secretary of War and General Halleck as a devoted adherent of General McClellan." (3)

In his autobiography Smith wrote: "Hooker was a man of a difficult character, and more dangerous. Some time in civil life he had sounded the depths of poverty from his own habits in California. He was thoroughly unprincipled and began at once, in any position, to pull down the man above him. With superb confidence in himself, good looks, and plausibility he finally pulled himself to the head of the army only to show that he had risen like other balloons to sink as soon as the weight was put on it which he as not fitted for carrying." (4)

While Baldy Smith was inactive, Hooker fought and lost the Battle of Chancellorsville. General Darius Couch, Hooker's second in command, refused to serve under Hooker any longer and was reassigned. Following the Battle of Chancellorsville Lee moved his army west and north for another invasion of North. On June 28, Lincoln picked Major General George Meade to replace Hooker as the commander of the Army of the Potomac. As noted earlier, James Hardie was given the assignment to notify Meade and Hooker of the change.

Then, in view of the danger of Lee's invasion threatening Pennsylvania, on June 10, the War Department established a new department, the Department of the Susquehanna. The new organization encompassed, "all the territory east of Johnstown and the Laurel Hill range of mountains." (5) On the same date, General Couch was appointed to head the new department. (6)

Smith was quick to offer his services to defend Pennsylvania and was willing to serve as a lieutenant. General Couch responded to his offer and had Smith busy assisting in the defenses of Harrisburg and organizing the New York and Pennsylvania militia. (7) On June 25 Couch assigned Brigadier General Smith to command "all the troops in the department on the south side of the Susquehanna River in the vicinity of Harrisburg." (8)

July 1 the battle of Gettysburg began. That day, Baldy Smith led a brigade of the New York National Guard and a brigade of the Pennsylvania militia to Carlisle. He found that Carlisle had been evacuated by the Confederates and started his command toward Mt. Holly Springs. About a mile and a half out of Carlisle, he learned that Confederate cavalry had appeared near the city and he returned to defend it. (9) The cavalry belonged to Stuart's command. Confederate cavalry chief, J.E.B. Stuart (West Point 1854) had undertaken a controversial ride around the Union army and wound up near Carlisle on July 1. He was attempting to link up with Lee's army. The Rebels attacked but were driven off and did not damage the city. They did burn the government barracks, a lumber yard and the gas works. General Smith thought lightly of the affair, but the ladies of Carlisle were grateful that the Rebels were prevented from burning the city. As a result, they presented General Smith with a beautifully engraved silver pitcher. (10) Meade's headquarters was pleased with Smith's efforts. General Gouverneur Warren (West Point 1850), who at that time was chief engineer of the Army of the Potomac, sent a message to Smith, "We are all much pleased with the way you behaved at Harrisburg bridge and Carlisle. It was a great help to us." (11)

From that point on the events that occurred were nightmares to General Smith. He and his militia remained at Carlisle on July 2 and 3 as the Battle of Gettysburg raged. While at Carlisle, Smith learned there was a road to Pine Grove Furnace and a way to get on Lee's line of communications. Smith proposed that he attack Lee's where he was vulnerable. General Couch agreed with Smith's plans and wired him on July 4 "It appears that your movement through by Pine Grove as discussed will be *just the thing*." (12). As his command headed for Pine Grove Furnace on July 4 it was surprised to meet a Rebel escort and 2,000 Union prisoners who had been given their parole. Concerned that word of his strength and intentions might reach Lee. Smith stopped the escort and sent the parolees back to Harrisburg subject to the orders of the War Department. General Couch then wired General Meade that he had the parolees and would send them to camp at West Chester. (13) Secretary of War Stanton harassed Smith by charging him with disobeying orders by having accepted a number of paroled prisoners as members of his force. Stanton's information was wrong and his accusation was without foundation.

At Pine Grove Furnace, a piece of gear used to pull the artillery broke and was left behind. The gear had been improvised from farm machinery. After the campaign was over, Stanton charged Smith for disgracefully losing a piece of artillery. (14) Stanton made life difficult for Baldy Smith. This was no doubt due to Smith's prior association with McClellan and Franklin.

Stanton, in Washington, sent a wire at 11:30 A M. on July 4 to the Adjutant General Lorenzo Thomas (West Point 1823), who was at Harrisburg, "the delay of General Couch in not pushing Smith forward with more promptness to cooperate with Meade has occasioned some disappointment here. I hope it is susceptible of satisfactory explanation." (15) That same day Adjutant General Thomas wired Secretary of War Stanton that "General Smith has gone forward with all available force, and as troops can be organized they will be pushed on. The New York artillerists sent here are perfectly worthless." (16)

General Couch wired Stanton on July 4 in an effort to get Stanton to understand his situation. 'As yet, a few of the New York regiments will not be mustered for any period. Some of them came here to serve for thirty days, others for three months. The latter would only be mustered for thirty days seeing that the former had that privilege." He continued," I am aware of the necessity that existed in hurrying forward troops, but if the emergency continues, I beg that all troops be mustered before leaving their respective States." (17) Couch tried to get the Secretary of War to appreciate that he was receiving untrained and unorganized men.

Initially, Couch's command was independent of Meade's Army of the Potomac. General Couch envisioned a role for Smith and his division completely different from that held by Meade. Smith was trapped in the middle. Because of this the period from July 6 to July 15 was a trying time for Baldy Smith.

On July 5 Couch advised Meade that Smith "would endeavor to get in Lee's rear, but you must not expect that raw militia will kill a great many." (18) That same day, Adjutant General Thomas advised Secretary Stanton that Smith had been "fully instructed to operate on the enemy's flank." (19) Then, on July 6, Meade instructed Smith to come to Gettysburg and guard the city and the hospitals while the enemy was near. (20) Couch countermanded Meade's order directing Smith not to join Meade. (21) That same day Halleck placed Couch under Meade and added, "His orders will be obeyed." (22) Baldy Smith did not want to serve under Meade and wired Couch "If you send an order for this command to report to Meade will you at the same time order me to return to you, leaving Knipe in command. You can appreciate how unpleasant it would be for me to serve under existing conditions with the Army of the Potomac." (23)

Meade wired Smith on July 7 to send one regiment to Gettysburg, and continue the pursuit of the enemy with the rest of his command, (24) Smith arrived in Waynesborough, Pennsylvania on July 8 and reported to Meade "My command is an incoherent mass . . . . they cannot be maneuvered and as a command is quite helpless, excepting in the kind of duty I have kept them on in the mountains. I have about 4,000 men, and I suppose 2,000 have straggled since I left Carlisle." (25)

From July 9 until July 13, Smith operated without specific orders from Meade or Couch even though he had repeatedly asked for them. (26) During the period he was at Waynesborough, Smith wired Meade, "I fear, if I am kept here to make a long march, I shall not be able to get into the fight." (27) He and his command finally arrived at Beaver Creek, near Hagerstown, Maryland, on, July 11. Smith was correct. He and his division did not get to the fight before Lee escaped and crossed the Potomac the night of July 13. (28)

President Lincoln was furious about Lee's escape. He wrote former Secretary of War Cameron, "I would give much to be relieved of the impression that Meade, Couch, and Smith, and all, since the battle of Gettysburg, have striven only to get Lee over the river without a fight." (29) Lincoln offered no basis for his criticism of Smith. The general's actions indicate that the criticism was not warranted. It appears Smith's earlier relations with McClellan still haunted him.

General Meade issued Special Orders No. 190 dated July 15, 1863 relieving General Smith and his command from further service with the Army of the Potomac and returning them to General Couch's command. The order read, "The major general commanding thanks Brigadier-General Smith and his troops for the zeal and promptitude which, amid no little privations, have marked their efforts to render this army all the assistance in their power . . ." (30) In contrast to the views in Washington General, Meade appreciated Smith's efforts

CHAPTER 16

Aftermath of the Gettysburg Campaign:
Politics and Command
July 15-August 26 1863

General Meade wired General Couch on July 14. He explained that, "The enemy evacuated last night the very strong position he occupied yesterday . . . . I am about moving down the river to cross at Berlin, and move down the Loudoun Valley. I wish to take every available man with me now with my army. At the same time I think Hagerstown ought to be occupied and the river watched, till we know what has become of Lee. If you can do this with the force under your command, you will render me an essential service. I have directed General Smith to report to you for instructions, as the time of his men is so nearly out." (1) Couch ordered Smith to carry out Meade's request. (2)

On July 17, Meade ordered Smith to move 200 Rebel sick and wounded out of Williamsport to Hagerstown and make them prisoners of war. In addition, Smith was directed to send a force to Williamsport large enough, "to prevent any communications between the rebels there and the rebel forces in Virginia." (3)

Prior to these actions the draft riots erupted on July 13, primarily in New York City, Governor Horatio Seymour of New York had openly opposed the draft and had refused to meet with Secretary Stanton to discuss it. The mayor of New York, Fernando Wood, opposed both the war and the draft. When the riots broke out, the city had only 1,500 police officers to deal with them. The militia and National Guard were with Couch. (4) Under orders from General Couch, General Smith sent the New York Militia and the 22nd Regiment, New York National Guard to return rapidly to New York to deal with the draft riots. The troops were held needlessly at Frederick, Maryland until all trouble was over. Smith was unable to understand Stanton's actions unless they were to punish the city.

Once the New York troops were on their way, General Smith hastened from his headquarters at Hagerstown to General Couch's headquarters at Chambersburg to ask Couch to let him go to New York City where he was wanted. He arrived at Couch's headquarters at 1:00 A.M., woke the general only to find that Couch had just received a telegram from Stanton demanding an explanation from Smith as to why he ordered the New York troops out of the field without authority. (5)

When General Smith moved his command into Maryland, as ordered by Meade and Couch, Secretary Stanton ordered Smith's arrest. Smith's offense was that he had taken his command beyond the border of Pennsylvania, and the militia had been called out solely to defend that state. General James H. Wilson, Smith's student at West Point, friend and biographer, reported the incident and indicated that General Couch, with difficulty, was able to get the order recalled (6)

Then Couch and Smith encountered two issues dealing with jurisdiction and rank. Both were very disturbing to Baldy Smith. Brigadier General Henry H. Lockwood (West Point 1836) assumed command of Maryland Heights and vicinity on July 18 per orders of General Meade. (7) The next day, General Meade placed Lockwood under Couch. (8) General Schenck was in command of the Middle Department with headquarters in Baltimore. Couch asked Halleck for clarification as to his jurisdiction and that of General Schenk, whose military department included all of Maryland. Halleck responded that the troops in the field from Couch's and Schenck's departments were placed under Couch by General Meade. (9) Presumably, that settled the issue, but Schenck continued to give orders to Lockwood and Lockwood virtually ignored Couch. (10)

On July 21 Couch informed Halleck that he had assigned General Smith responsibility for "all the troops from Maryland Heights to Clear Spring." (11) When General Lockwood learned that General Smith was to be his superior, he refused to report to him claiming that Smith was his junior in rank. (12) Lockwood appealed to Halleck who wrote to General Couch," You have no authority, so far as I am aware, to place a junior over a senior." (13) That eliminated Maryland Heights and Lockwood's 6,163 men from Smith's command. (14)

The act apparently was "the straw that broke the camel's back" for Baldy Smith. He wired General Couch on July 23 "Dear General: I have been trying to fulfill your wishes and do my duty here in a manner creditable to you and myself, and, now that obstacles are thrown in my way at every step, will you please relieve me from this embarrassing position by ordering me elsewhere? As Lee has fallen back, and as your militia here is getting mutinous in its resolves, I think you had better call back all your troops unless the department chooses to put this in your command, as it should do. I have no doubt that I rank General Lockwood, and if I do you might, by a messenger direct to Meade, set things to rights at once, but still I don't think *'le jeu vaut la chandelle'* (it is worth the effort), and my present position is simply insupportable, because I cannot give an order that I am certain that I have the power to force the execution of." (15)

General Couch asked Baldy to hold on for the present. (16) He did and things settled down for a while. (17) On August 3.General Halleck ordered General Couch to turn over all his troops in Maryland to Brigadier General Kelley, according to the new boundaries of the Department of West Virginia. (18) Orders were issued on August 26, 1863 "Brig. Gen. William F. Smith, commanding at Hagerstown, Md., is, at his own request, relieved from duty at that post and ordered to report to the Adjutant-General, U.S. Army, at Washington City for orders." (19) With the campaign over, Smith said that all he had to show for his labors in the Militia Campaign were the distortions and persecutions that followed him (20)

In sharp contrast to Stanton's attitude and actions, General Meade appreciated Smith's endeavors. In his report on the Gettysburg Campaign, he wrote," It is my duty as well as my pleasure, to call attention to the earnest efforts of cooperation on the part of Maj. Gen. D.N. Couch, commanding Department of the Susquehanna, and particularly his advance, 4,000 men, under Brig. Gen. W. F. Smith, who joined me at Boonesborough, just prior to the withdrawal of the Confederate army."

CHAPTER 17

Chattanooga
September 30-October 19, 1863

With the conclusion of the Gettysburg campaign Baldy Smith was sent to New York to await further orders. He fretted with inactivity and got help to obtain a new assignment. Three influential citizens of New York City, Alexander Hamilton, grandson of the first Secretary of the Treasury; W. Denning Duer, a prominent New York banker, and James T. Brady, a prominent New York lawyer and former associate of Secretary Stanton, went to Washington and asked Stanton to assign General Smith to active duty. Stanton then asked Smith where he'd like to be assigned and Smith replied that he would serve anywhere except the Department of the Gulf because of his history of malaria. After a few days, he received orders assigning him to the Department of the Gulf! That forced Smith to get a surgeon to certify that he could not serve in that climate. Finally, on September 5, he received orders to report to General Rosecrans, Commander of the Army of the Cumberland. (1)

Rosecrans and Confederate General Braxton Bragg (West Point 1837) fought battles in the Chickamauga Campaign starting in September 10 and ending on September 21 with a Union defeat. Following the decisive Battle of Chickamauga (September 20-21) Rosecrans retreated to Chattanooga, Tennessee. Bragg decided on the investment of the Union army. (2) At the end of the campaign, Rosecrans had only one route from the railhead at Stevenson, Alabama to supply his troops. (3) On October 1, Bragg sent his cavalry under General Joseph Wheeler (West Point 1859) in an attempt to sever Rosecrans' supply line. Wheeler was not completely successful, but he burned 300 Union wagons and captured 1,800 mules. Wheeler's men also "captured" Smith's baggage and Smith arrived in Chattanooga with only the clothes on his back. (4)

Rosecrans was at loss as to how to deal with the situation his army was in and spent his time writing his report defending his defeat at Chickamauga. C.A. Dana, who was Stanton's liaison with Rosecrans, reported this about Rosecrans on October 12, "His mind scatters; there is no system in the use of his busy days and sleepless nights . . . . he is a feeble commander . . . I consider this army to be very unsafe in his hands." (5)

The Army of the Cumberland was starving. Men were on half rations, the supply line was sixty miles long, animals pulling the supply wagons were so weak that their loads had to be lightened. The beef cattle that were driven those sixty miles were so worn down from the drive that the soldiers called them "dried beef." The Confederates outnumbered the Army of the Cumberland and their artillery and infantry controlled all the supply routes from Bridgeport to Chattanooga. Retreat was out of the question. A move toward Bridgeport would result in loss of life, loss of artillery, and possible surrender of the entire Army of the Cumberland. It would also mean the loss of East Tennessee which Lincoln felt was vital to the North.

Brigadier General Smith arrived at Chattanooga on September 30 1863. Rosecrans had to decide how to use his services. There were two choices, as a division commander or as chief engineer of the Army of the Cumberland. Rosecrans fortuitously chose the latter; it was a decision that saved the besieged army. Smith's appointment was effective on October 3. (6) Orders were issued on October 10 confirming his appointment and placing all troops on engineering duty and all engineering operations under his control. (7) Rosecrans issued another order on October 9 directing division topographical officers to report their work on a daily basis to General Smith.

The topography around Chattanooga was all-important in saving the Army of the Cumberland. The Confederates had made maximum use of the topography in their siege of the Union army. The question was whether Smith and the Union army could use topography to escape from the trap they were in.

Chattanooga is on the south side of the Tennessee River at the end of a valley through which runs the Chattanooga Creek. The Tennessee

River runs nearly due west. To the east of the valley is Missionary Ridge that rises to elevation of five hundred to eight hundred feet. It sets back from the river. Opposite to and west of the city is Lookout Mountain; it touches the river and rises perpendicularly 2,200 feet. West of Lookout Mountain is Lookout Valley and west of that is the Raccoon Mountain (8) General U.S. Grant wrote, "The intrenched line of the enemy commenced on the north end of Missionary Ridge and extended along the crest for some distance south, thence across Chattanooga Valley to Lookout Mountain. Lookout Mountain was also fortified and held by the enemy, who also kept troops in Lookout Valley and on Raccoon Mountain, with pickets extending down the river so as to command the road on the south bank and render it useless to us. In addition to this there was an intrenched line in Chattanooga Valley extending from the river east of the town to Lookout Mountain to make the investment complete . . . . Practically the Army of the Cumberland was besieged. The enemy, with his cavalry north of the river, had stopped the passing of a train loaded with ammunition and medical supplies. The Union army was short of both, not having enough ammunition for a day's fighting." (9)

Baldy Smith tried to convince Rosecrans that the army could not subsist "during the winter without opening the river, as the roads over the mountains would become nearly impassible after the autumn rains set in." (10) Rosecrans stubbornly insisted that such was not the case and refused to listen. (11) Back in Washington, things were in an uproar. Lincoln described Rosecrans as "confused and stunned like a duck hit on the head." (12) On the night of September 23 Stanton called a meeting to deal with the pending disaster. The decision was made to send two corps from the Army of the Potomac—the Eleventh Corps under Oliver Otis Howard (West Point 1854) and the Twelfth Corps under Henry Slocum—to the rescue. Joseph Hooker was assigned to lead the expedition. From September 23 to October 6 in the first mass movement of troops in history (13) approximately 15,000 men were moved from Washington to Bridgeport on the Tennessee. (14)

General Rosecrans indicated he planned to order Hooker to open the river by driving the Confederates from Lookout Mountain. Smith reasoned that this would be a move made in desperation for the Confederates could contest Hooker's approach through the mountain passes and crush him in Lookout Valley before the Army of the

Cumberland could help him. (15) General Smith approached General Rosecrans on October 18 and told him he wanted to see if there was a better way of proceeding. He invited Rosecrans to join him on a trip to study the country on the next day. Rosecrans agreed, but as they started out, Rosecrans stopped at the hospital to visit friends and Smith went on without him. Smith went to Moccasin Point and studied the banks carefully. There on the northwest bank he met the commander of a section of the Eighteenth Ohio Battery of artillery guarding Brown's Ferry. Baldy reported that he "walked down to the river bank and sat here for an hour scanning the hills, the gap, the road through it, and the smoke of the picket guard camp fires, which were some distance back from the river." (16) He returned to camp convinced that there was a practical way out of their situation and was prepared to brief General Rosecrans on his plan. Upon returning to camp he found that a telegram had been received relieving Rosecrans and replacing him with George Thomas (West Point 1840). The administration had also created a new department, the Department of the Mississippi, encompassing the departments of the Cumberland, the Ohio, and the Tennessee, and appointed U.S. Grant to command it. (17)

Smith now had to sell his plan to Thomas and Grant.

CHAPTER 18

"The Cracker Line"
October 20-28, 1863

U.S. Grant had been victorious at Vicksburg and was expected to perform miracles by rescuing the Army of the Cumberland and saving Eastern Tennessee for the Union. Secretary Stanton was so exercised about the situation at Chattanooga that he met General Grant at Indianapolis on October 17, 1863 and traveled with him to Louisville. On the train, Stanton handed Grant two orders and gave him a choice. The orders were identical except in one particular. Both created the Military Division of the Mississippi composed of the Departments of the Ohio, the Cumberland, and the Tennessee and all the territory from the Alleghenies to the Mississippi north of General Nathaniel Bank's command in the southwest. One of the orders left Rosecrans in command of the Army of the Cumberland, the other replaced Rosecrans with Major General George Thomas. Grant chose the latter. (1)

While at Louisville, Stanton received a dispatch from his assistant, Dana that indicated Rosecrans was preparing to retreat. Grant was visiting friends in the city and Stanton frantically sent people out to locate him. When the general heard the news he issued orders assuming the command of the military division, and he relieved Rosecrans and assigned Thomas to the command of the Army of the Cumberland. Grant later wrote that a retreat would have meant the loss of a strategic location, all the artillery of the Army of the Cumberland, and the annihilation of that army either by capture or demoralization. (2) Grant promptly sent an order to Thomas directing him to hold Chattanooga "at all hazards." Thomas replied, "We will hold this town till we starve." (3)

Upon arrival in Chattanooga, General Smith made a thorough inspection of the topography of the area. He was convinced from his examination that the only way to supply the army was to open the river. That was the sole option the Union had to shorten the distance to be traveled from Bridgeport to Chattanooga. (4)

On October 24 Grant arrived in Chattanooga. He met with most of the general officers of the Army of the Cumberland. Baldy Smith briefed him on the situation. Later, General Grant wrote, "General Smith explained the situation of the two armies and the topography of the country so plainly that I could see it without an inspection." (5) From that time on, Smith was an indispensable member of Grant's command.

He described the plan he conceived. "If that ridge of hills [held by the Rebels on the south side of the river] could be surprised and held, and a bridge built there, then we could throw troops into Lookout Valley faster than the rebels, and any forces disputing the passes leading through the mountains to Bridgeport would have us on their flank; if they made a fight against our force in our direction [they would find] Hooker's force coming at right angles [against them]." (6)

To attack the Rebel force, Smith proposed building a pontoon bridge at Brown's Ferry He would do this with pontoons floated from Chattanooga to the landing site. The pontoons would carry one half of the attack force. These troops would be supported by others marched across Moccasin Point from Chattanooga. Hooker's men would seize Lookout Valley and join forces with the Army of the Cumberland to attack the Confederate forces south of the river. If successful, these actions would open the river from Bridgeport to Brown's Ferry. From Brown's Ferry the supplies would then be transported by land across Moccasin Point and the bridge to Chattanooga.

Baldy created a whirlwind of activity to carry out his plan. U.S. Grant wrote, "I found that he had established a sawmill on the banks of the river, by utilizing an old engine found in the neighborhood, and by rafting logs from the north side of the river above, had got out lumber and completed pontoons and roadway plank for a second bridge, one flying bridge being there already . . . . In addition to this he had far under way a steamer for plying between Chattanooga and Bridgeport whenever he might get possession of the river." (7)

Smith had gotten General Thomas' approval for the plan before Genial Grant arrived. On the 24 of October Generals Grant, Thomas and Smith made an inspection of the routes of attack. Upon return to Chattanooga, Grant was prepared to act. If successful, "The Cracker Line" across Moccasin Point would soon be open. General Grant was enthusiastic about Smith's plan. He wrote "General Smith had been so instrumental in preparing for the move I was now about to make, and so clear in his judgment about the manner of making it, that I deemed it but just to him that he should take command of the troops detailed to execute the design although he was then acting as a staff officer and not in command of troops." (8)

On the night of the 24th Grant issued orders for the movement. Smith was given command of two brigades, one under General Turchin and one under General Hazen (West Point 1855). Smith was to build the bridge at Brown's Ferry, seize the hills there and join with Hooker's forces. Hooker was to cross the river at Bridgeport, drive the Confederates away from the river and join Smith at Brown's Ferry. General Palmer (West Point 1846), with a division of the Fourteenth Corps, Army of the Cumberland, was to march down the stream, cross over at Whitesides and hold the road after Hooker's men had passed. (9)

General Hazen had the most difficult and riskiest assignment in the entire operation; one that required superb planning and precise execution. Hazen learned of his task the morning of October 25. He was to organize 50 squads of 1 officer and 24 men to embark on pontoon boats, float down the river 9 miles, land on the left bank, attack the enemy at Brown's Ferry and hold the position there. He would be rapidly supported by the remainder of his brigade and Turchin's brigade under General Smith, who would march across Moccasin Point and cross at Brown's Ferry on the pontoon boats brought there by Hazen. The movement was to start before daylight on October 27.

General Smith took General Hazen to Brown's Ferry on the 26 where they carefully inspected the place where Hazen's men were to land. Later, Hazen selected the officers who would command the boats, and after instructing them on their assignments, took them to Brown's Ferry and reviewed every aspect of the proposed landing with them.

At exactly 3:00 A.M. on October 27, the flotilla of 50 boats moved out. They passed the Rebel pickets without being discovered. At the end of the 9 mile journey, the Rebels at Brown's Ferry fired a volley but it did no damage. The attack force disembarked and met with resistance which was soon overcome. (10)

General Smith, the rest of Hazen's men and Turchin's brigade marched across Moccasin Point at 6:30 P.M. on October 26 and bivouacked in the woods near Brown's Ferry. They were in a position where they could rapidly support Hazen's attack force. Hazen's men landed at 5:00 A.M. By 7:00 A.M. all of Smith's force had been ferried across the river and had fortified the heights commanding the ferry. By 1.00 P.M., the pontoon bridge was completed making it possible to rapidly bring more reinforcements as needed. (11)

Hooker crossed the Tennessee River at Bridgeport on October 26. The next day he started the march through the Raccoon Mountains and Lookout Valley to Brown's Ferry. Resistance was light and when rebels were encountered, they fled. (12) General Hazen was able report at 3:45 P.M. on October 28, "General Hooker's column is coming up from Lookout Valley [and is] within a quarter of a mile from our position."(13)

C. A. Dana, Stanton's assistant, wired Secretary Stanton at 5:00 P.M. on October 28, "Everything perfectly successful. The river is now open and a short and good road in our possession along the south shore. We had an insignificant skirmish near Wauhatchie. The great success, however, is General Smith's operation at the mouth of Lookout Valley. Its brilliancy cannot be exaggerated." (14)

CHAPTER 19

The Chattanooga Campaign
October 28-December 4, 1863

A new mood, one stemming from success, dominated the headquarters of the Army of the Cumberland the evening of October 28. General Thomas would soon issue a congratulatory order thanking Generals Smith, Hazen and Turchin and their commands for reopening the river and saving the Army of the Cumberland. (1)

Then General Butterfield, Hooker's chief of staff, arrived and reported Hooker's presence in the area. He also reported that Hooker had not placed his troops in a defensive position to ward off an enemy attack. When General Smith heard Butterfield's report he was alarmed and went to General Reynolds, Thomas' chief of staff, and urged him to get Thomas to direct Hooker to put his men in good defensive positions. Smith was certain that Longstreet would attack Hooker and reasoned that if Longstreet were successful, the army would lose everything it had gained. Apparently, Reynolds neglected to pass Smith's concerns to Thomas. (2) However, General Hazen went to Hooker with the same advice. Hooker refused to change his orders and left his men in vulnerable positions. (3)

Shortly after midnight on October 28, Longstreet launched an attack on General Geary's men near Wauhatchie. The fierce fight that ensued lasted three hours. Finally, the Rebels retreated. The fight cost Geary 216 casualties, 36 killed, 174 wounded, and 6 missing. Most tragic was the loss of Geary's own son, Lieutenant E. R. Geary who was killed while manning artillery in Knaps Battery. In his report, General Geary wrote, "Many regrets follow those brave young hearts to their soldier graves, succumbing, in the hour of youth's promising, brightest manhood to the hostility of our country's enemy. In the latter named, I may be permitted to remark, I experience, in conjunction with the keen regrets of a commanding officer for a worthy officer, the pangs of a father's grief for a cherished son, whose budding worth in wealth of intellect and courage was filling full the cup of paternal pride." (4) On October 29, at Smith's instigation, General Grant ordered General Smith to lay out lines for Hooker to take up and fortify. Once completed, the danger from a possible successful Rebel attack was over. (5)

Also that day, October 29, Stanton's assistant Dana wired Stanton, that General Grant "wishes to have both Hooker and Slocum removed from his command and that the Eleventh and Twelfth Corps consolidated under Howard. He would himself order Hooker and Slocum away, but hesitates because they have just been sent here by the President . . . . Hooker has behaved badly ever since his arrival and Slocum has just sent in a very disorderly communication, stating that when he came here, it was under promise that he should not have to serve under Hooker, who he neither regards with confidence as an officer nor respects as a man. Altogether, Grant feels that their presence here is replete with both trouble and danger." (6) Nothing happened to Grant's request.

Once the Tennessee River was reopened, the priorities were: supplying the troops with food, clothing and ammunition; attacking Bragg's army; and making sure that Burnside and East Tennessee were safe.

On the way to Chattanooga, General Grant ordered that a good supply of vegetables and small rations be readied to send to Chattanooga when the river and roads were reopened. (7) Smith had repaired an old steamboat at Chattanooga and it was sent to Bridgeport right after the river was clear. It returned promptly with provisions for "a very joyous army." (8) The steamboat Paint Rock was sent from Bridgeport to Brown's Ferry; it was capable of carrying 200 tons of freight. (9) The condition of the Army of the Cumberland improved rapidly as the troops were quickly back on full rations. General Grant wrote, 'The men were soon reclothed and well fed, and an abundance of ammunition was brought up, and a cheerfulness prevailed not heretofore enjoyed in many weeks. Neither officers nor men looked upon themselves as doomed; the weak and languid appearance of the troops, visible before, disappeared at once." (10)

From the time he was assigned to head the Military Division of Mississippi, General Grant was pressured to act to save Eastern Tennessee. (11) Burnside was at Knoxville with a force of 12,000. (12) On November 4, Longstreet was detached from Bragg's army and sent with 15,000 infantry and artillery and 5,000 cavalry to go against Burnside. The authorities in Washington plied Grant with dispatches about saving East Tennessee faster than ever. (13)

On November 5, Dana wired Secretary Stanton, "Grant and Thomas considering plan proposed by W. F. Smith to advance our pickets on the left to Citico Creek, about a mile in front of the position they have occupied from the first, and threaten the seizure of the northwest extremity of Missionary Ridge. This action, in connection with our present demonstration in Lookout Valley, will compel them to concentrate and come back from Burnside and fight here." (14) Grant accepted Smith's plan and peremptorily ordered Thomas to carry it out. (15)

General Thomas, after receiving the order, indicated that he felt he was too weak to do as ordered. He appealed to General Smith for help. When the two of them got a good view of Bragg's lines and the topography of the area, they could see that the lines stretched too far for Thomas' men to outflank them. Smith then went to Grant, reported their findings, and recommended postponement of the movement until Sherman (West Point 1840) arrived. Grant reluctantly agreed. (16) (17)

In his autobiography, Smith noted that Grant's order to Thomas was "a very general one" and asked Grant if he intended to give more detailed instructions. According to Smith, Grant replied "that when he had confidence enough in the man to leave him in command of an army he had confidence enough to leave the details to him." (18) This philosophy, while appropriate, would have terrible consequences later at Cold Harbor when subordinate commanders failed to research the field and devise an intelligent plan of attack.

Sherman led the Fifteenth and Seventeenth Corps to Chattanooga by way of Bridgeport. He reached Chattanooga on November 15, the two corps would follow. He soon learned that he would have the key role in the attack of Bragg's army. (19) The plan of attack, initially developed by General Smith and adopted by General Grant, was based on attacking Bragg's right and seizing Tunnel Hill. If successful, this would move

Bragg away from his communications and his line of retreat. Sherman was on the left side of the Union line and was given this most important role in the movement. One of his divisions, Osterhaus' was to march up Lookout Valley, threaten Trenton and a pass at Lookout Mountain. This was to be done in daylight where the enemy could observe the action. At night, the division was to march back, cross the river at Brown's Ferry and join Sherman. Thomas, in the middle of the Union line, was to threaten the center of Bragg's line, and be prepared to assist Sherman. Hooker, on the right of the Union line, was to threaten Lookout Mountain and do whatever was possible. (20) (21).

On November 12 Grant issued an order making General Smith chief engineer of the Military Division of Mississippi. This action officially elevated Smith to a position on Grant's staff. The record indicates that his actual role was much broader. (2)

Once the planning was completed, Baldy Smith returned to his whirlwind of activity. His first task was to strengthen the defenses at Chattanooga. This was done by November 21. Bridges were needed and he had two sawmills operating day and night. Bridges were to be thrown across the Chattanooga Creek, the Citico Creek, the West Chickamauga Creek, the South Chickamauga Creek, and the Little Tennessee. The most important bridge was the one to cross the Tennessee River where the width of the river was 1,240 feet. (23)

Sherman's orders were for the Fifteenth Corps, reinforced by a division of the Army of the Cumberland, to cross the Tennessee at the mouth of the East Chickamauga, advance and take possession of the end of Missionary Ridge; Grant's orders read," General William Smith will give you the detailed arrangements for crossing over . . . ." (24) Osterhaus' division was not able to cross at Brown's Ferry because the bridge broke. He was sent to reinforce Hooker. (25) On November 23, Sherman reported that his three divisions lay behind the hills opposite the mouth of the Chickamauga Creek. (26)

Smith sent a brigade of infantry in 116 pontoon boats to land on the bank of the river at the mouth of creek, seize the landing place, hold it and construct the bridge for Sherman's troops. The soldiers used the pontoons they arrived in to build the bridge. (27) Sherman wrote about the movement, "the whole [operation] planned and supervised by General William F. Smith in person . . . . I have never beheld any work done so quietly, so well, and I doubt if the history of war can show a bridge of that extent (viz. 1,300 feet) laid so well and so noiselessly in so short a time. I attribute it to the genius and intelligence of General William F. Smith." (28)

At daylight of November 24 8,000 troops were across the river and in line of battle. Brigadier General James Wilson, Smith's former pupil, brought up the steamer Dunbar and ferried another 5,000 men, a battery of artillery, and the horses of the generals and their staffs. Maps of the battlefield were prepared under Smith's direction by officers of the U.S. Coast Survey were distributed and used by the artillery to determine distance and heights from artillery positions. (29)

By noon of November 24, Sherman had his entire command across the river. His men marched from the river at 1:00 P.M. gained the foothills and by 3:30 P.M. had gained two high points which he fortified. (30) General Thomas, in the center of the line, had driven the enemy's pickets on November 23 and had captured the Confederate's first line. Hooker, on the right, drove the enemy from his rifle pits on the northern extremity of Lookout Mountain. On the night of the 24 Grant had an unbroken line from the north end of Lookout Mountain, through Chattanooga Valley, to the north end of Missionary Ridge. (31)

The second day of the battle, Hooker was ordered to attack and carry the Rossville Gap on Missionary Ridge, while Sherman, facing severe fighting, attempted to reach the crest of Missionary Ridge. (32) Grant, Thomas, Smith and others were at Orchard Knob in the center of the line. Uncertain about Sherman's success, Grant ordered Thomas to attack and then directed Smith to give the order to Brigadier General Absalom Baird (West Point 1849). Smith said, "When I delivered the order [to attack] to General Baird, he asked me what he was to do if he carried the rifle pits and I told him I had received no instructions on that point." (33) Smith continued "I would not look at it [the attack] for I thought they would be terribly beaten, and I turned my back to the magnificent effort of the American soldier. Finally, a cheer came and our flag crowned the heights and stayed there, and the battle was won. The ridge was carried by the light of the setting sun on a short November day."(34)

Smith's original plan for the battle, adopted by Grant, had not been followed. Osterhaus had not been able to use the bridge at Brown's Ferry and Sherman had not been able to meet his objectives due to stiff opposition. (35) Grant had skillfully modified the plan to meet these changes. (36) Hooker led the pursuit of Bragg's army, and was "badly handled" at Ringgold. Grant and his staff followed the pursuit, accompanying Thomas' command. Thomas' troops were in no condition to pursue and Grant gave up the chase and turned to the effort to save Burnside. (37) At the end of the pursuit, Grant and his staff stayed at the house of a local citizen. Smith wrote, ". . . . I remember the disgusted look the man had when Grant paid him in Confederate money." (38)

Lincoln, Stanton, and Halleck knew that Longstreet and Wheeler had been detached from Bragg's army in early November to operate against Burnside in East Tennessee and they put great pressure on Grant to help Burnside. (39) (40) Burnside repeatedly indicated in his dispatches that he could hold his position as long as his ammunition held out. (41)

General Smith had no faith in Burnside's assurances and his ability to plan and defend Knoxville and Eastern Tennessee. His evaluation was based upon his experience under Burnside at the Battle of Fredericksburg. In early November, Smith conferred with Grant and discussed Burnside's shortcomings. He urged Grant to send someone to Knoxville to tell Burnside what to do. General Grant proposed sending Smith to command there, but Smith pointed out that he was a brigadier general and his rank precluded such action. Grant then sent Stanton's' assistant, C. A. Dana and Brig. General James Wilson to Burnside as his special messengers. (42) They arrived at Burnside's headquarters on or before November 13. (43)

General Smith wrote that he later learned that Lt. Col. Charles Loring, Burnside's inspector general and Lt. Col. Lewis Richmond, Burnside's adjutant general, using Burnside's name, had saved Burnside's command while Burnside was far in the rear and knew little about what was happening. (44) After Bragg was defeated, Longstreet remained in front of Knoxville until December 4. When he learned that three Union columns were on their way to Knoxville, he retreated. (45) East Tennessee had been saved.

CHAPTER 20

Accolades for General Smith, Hooker's Criticism
December 5, 1863-March 26, 1864

Smith's accomplishments in late 1863 won him high praise. In 1864, decisions were made about his future that led to personal disaster. The records speak for themselves.

November 12, 1863   U.S. Grant to Secretary Stanton

"I would respectfully recommend that Brig. Gen. W.F. Smith be placed first on the list for promotion to the rank of major-general. He is possessed of one of the clearest military heads in the army; is very practical and industrious. No man in the service is better qualified than he for our largest commands." (1)

November 18, 1863   Edwin M. Stanton to Major-General Butler

"The services of W.F. Smith, now chief of engineers in the Army of the Cumberland, are indispensable in that command and it will be impossible to assign him to your department." (2)

November 20, 1863   Geo. H Thomas to Brigadier General Thomas,
                     Adjutant General, U.S. Army

"I have the honor to recommend for favorable consideration the following-named officers of this army, and respectfully urge their promotions for the following reasons:

Brig. Gen. W.F. Smith, for the industry and energy displayed by him from the time of his first reporting for duty at these headquarters; in organizing the engineer department, and, for his skillful execution of the movements at Brown's Ferry, Tenn. on the night of October 26, 1863, in surprising the enemy and throwing a pontoon bridge across the Tennessee at that point—a vitally important service necessary to the opening of communication between Bridgeport and Chattanooga." (3)

November 30, 1863 U.S. Grant to His Excellency Abraham Lincoln

"In a previous letter addressed to the Secretary of War, I recommended Brig. Gen. W. F. Smith for promotion. Recent events have entirely satisfied me of his great capabilities and merits, and I hasten to renew the recommendation and to urge it. The interests of the public service would be better subserved by this promotion than the interests of General Smith himself. My reasons for writing this letter now is to ask that W. F. Smith's name be placed first on the list for promotion of all those previously recommended by me." (4)

December 1, 1863   C.A. Dana to Maj. Gen. U.S. Grant

"To my suggestion that the surest way to getting the rebels altogether out of East Tennessee is to be found in the Army of the Potomac, the reply is, that is true, but from that army nothing is to be hoped under its present commander. This naturally led to your second proposition, namely, that either Sherman or W.F. Smith should be put in command of that army. To this the answer is such as to leave little doubt in my mind that the second of these officers will be appointed to that post. Both Secretary of War and General Halleck said to me that so long as a fortnight before my arrival they had come to the conclusion that when a change should be made General W. F. Smith would be the best person to try.

Some doubts which they seemed to have respecting his disposition and personal character I think I was able to clear up. Secretary of War has also directed me to inform him that he is to be promoted on the first vacancy. President, Secretary of War, and General Halleck agree with you in thinking it would be, on the whole, much better to select him than Sherman. As yet, however, nothing has been decided upon, and you will understand I have somewhat exceeded my instructions from the Secretary of War in his communication, especially in the second branch of it, but it seems to me necessary that you should know all the particulars." (5)

January 13, 1864   U.S. Grant to Maj. Gen. H.W. Halleck

"If General Foster (West Point 1846) is relieved General McPherson (West Point 1953) or General Schofield (West Point 1853) would suit me to fill his place, but both are ranked by generals already in the Department of the Ohio. I would recommend, therefore, the appointment of General W.F. Smith, to major general and rank dated back to his first appointment and he be given the command. If it is in contemplation to give General Smith a higher command, either of the officers named or General Parke (West Point 1849) will suit me." (6)

January 13, 1864   H.W. Halleck to Maj. Gen. U.S. Grant

"I have just received your telegram, recommending the appointment of Brig. Gen. W.F. Smith to a major generalcy. Your former recommendation was submitted to the Secretary of War, and I think the appointment will be made as soon as there is a vacancy. Not only is there no vacancy now, but by some error more than the number authorized by law were made last summer, and some major generals now in service must be dropped." (7)

February 23, 1864   Joseph Hooker, Major General to
                     Hon. E.M. Stanton

"Permit me to call your attention to the above choice gems from the newspaper world [not found]. The former was cut from a letter written from here November 29, by C.D Brigham and appeared in the New York Tribune on the 9 of December, and the latter was kindly sent me from the office of the New York Times where it had been sent by the same individual, Brigham. . . . . I called on this correspondent, Brigham, to furnish me with the name of the individual whom he styles, "one who has a right to criticize." On making inquiries I find that his bosom friend while at Chattanooga was Brig. Gen. W.F. Smith, the officer I applied to have assigned to the Ninth Corps at the time it was removed from the Army of the Potomac, as I recognized in him the evil genius of Franklin, Brooks, and Newton . . . . The point of all [this criticism of Hooker's performance at Ringgold] was to shut me out of the fight. Grant's object being to give the éclat to his old army, and Smith's, if he really had anything to do with it, to exclude your humble servant . . . . As for Smith, he has an ascendancy over Grant, who is simple minded, but it will not be likely to be long lived . . . . Grant applied for a brigadier-general [Smith] to be put in command of a department who has never fought a battle; at least so I am informed . . . . It is the first time, so far as I know, that my humanity as a soldier has been assailed by any one, outside or inside my command, and now only by a thief and a liar." (8)

[Hooker alleged that Grant and Smith stole some of the glory due him and that Smith lied about the role he had in planning the Battle of Chattanooga.]

March 9, 1864   Senate Confirmation

At U.S. Grant's insistence, the Senate confirmed W.F. Smith as a major general.

March 11-26, 1864   Excerpts from the Autobiography of Major
General William F. Smith, 1861-1864

"After General Grant had received the opportunity as Lieutenant General [March 12, 1864] he wrote to suggest my name (among others I believe) for the commanding general of the Army of the Potomac. While in Washington after General Grant's arrival there I received two or three letters from members of the old staff in Nashville congratulating me, as General Grant had written that he was going to have me appointed to the Army of the Potomac. A few days after arriving in Washington Grant visited the Army of the Potomac [March 11, 1864] and insisted on my going with him. I went very reluctantly and on the way down to Culpepper Court House met for a while with Colonel [John A.] Rawlins,

Grant's Chief of Staff. I said to him that there would be no change in the command of the Army of the Potomac and I wished him during the campaign to keep certain points in view. He interrupted me, and said he did not agree with me and my assertion—that the day before he had been with the Secretary of War and General Grant and the Secretary had said, 'General Grant, you are going to the Army of the Potomac and you will find a very weak irresolute man there and my advice is to make a change at once.' General Grant asked how it would do to bring one of his western generals in to fill the place mentioning [General James B] McPherson's name. To this the Secretary replied "It will not answer—the army must be commanded by a man who had served with it and I advise you to take General 'Baldy' Smith who is well known there and has the confidence of all. After Rawlins finished I said, I was 'confident there will be no change and hope you will remember what I say to you about the campaign.'

"That night I spent with the Sixth Corps and the next morning General Meade went with us to Washington, assured in his position." (9)

March 26, 1864   *Stanton*, Lincoln's Secretary of War by Fletcher Pratt

When Grant came back [from a visit with Sherman in the West] on the twenty-sixth [of March], he set up headquarters at Culpepper Court House, and the conferences began—with Lincoln, Stanton, and Halleck . . . . Pratt reported the following about the conferences in his book

"Next officers. The little Aulic council seems to have agreed that Sigel and Butler were dubious as commanders. But their efforts were diversionary, and both had an importance well beyond the downright military. Butler claimed to be the senior major-general of the army and said he could prove it by the almanac; was so potent a political personality that to remove him would be courting opposition in country and Congress just when such opposition could least be afforded, at the outset of a Presidential campaign. Lincoln called him 'the damnedest scoundrel that ever lived, but in the infinite mercy of Providence, also the damnedest fool.' He could be propped up with good corps commanders and might even accomplish something."

Grant put in a bid for his old friend Baldy Smith, whom the Senate had refused to confirm as a major general sometime before; Lincoln and Stanton would work out the confirmation, and he would have a corps under Butler—"just the right man". (10) (Note: As indicated above, Smith's promotion was effective on March 9, 1864.)

CHAPTER 21

Butler—The Damnedest Scoundrel
March 3, 1864-April 29, 1864

General Smith accompanied General Grant to Washington and arrived there on March 3, 1864. (1) He expected to have a major role in the coming campaign but things quickly turned sour for him.

In order for Smith to be appointed to a significant position, army or corps command, he had to be a major general, the highest rank in the army at that time. General Grant pushed the nomination through despite strenuous opposition. He wrote, "I found a decided prejudice against his confirmation by a majority of the Senate, but I insisted that his services had been such that he should be rewarded." (2) The Senate approval was completed without referring the nomination to the military committee. (3) Grant also wrote in his Memoirs, "My wishes were now reluctantly complied with, and I assigned him to the command of one of the corps under General Butler. I was not long in finding that the objections to Smith's promotion were well founded." (4) General Grant offered no explanation for that comment; i.e. the events that caused the change in his attitude and the times they occurred.

While Smith was with Grant at Nashville in the winter of 1863-1864, he had drawn up plans for the Union armies' campaigns for 1864. Grant embodied Smith's plans in letters sent to Halleck on January 15, 1864. (5) and January 19, 1864. (6) For the Army of the Potomac, Grant proposed abandoning the previously attempted line to Richmond, striking the railroad at Weldon, using New Bern, North Carolina, as a base of operations. Grant wrote, "It [the plan] would draw the enemy from campaigns of their own choosing, and for which they are not prepared, to new lines of operation never expected to be necessary." (7) Smith felt that Halleck killed his plan and did so while he was still general-in-chief. (8)

General Smith continued to advocate his plan to General Grant and did so by having his friend, General Wilson give it to him. In the process, he alienated Grant's chief of staff, Brigadier General John Rawlins, and may have alienated Grant too. (9)

As indicated earlier, Grant arrived in Washington with the intent of naming General Smith to replace General Meade. He continued to advocate this action until after he conferred with General Meade on March 10, 1864. The next day, March 11, General Meade accompanied Generals Grant and Smith back to Washington assured that he would retain his position as commander of the Army of the Potomac. (10)

That same day, Meade appeared before the Joint Committee on the Conduct of the War and defended his actions at Gettysburg. The Joint Committee and Meade's enemies—Secretary Chase, Generals Hooker, Sickles, Doubleday, Birney, Butterfield and Albion Howe (West Point 1841)—were out to destroy him. (11) Had they succeeded, Lincoln would have lost control of appointments to the major command in the East, and Chase and the Radical Republicans would probably have demanded that Hooker be restored to the position he once held.

President Lincoln expressed his position on the leadership of the Army of the Potomac in August, 1864 when a change of command for Meade was under consideration. Lincoln felt that the public would not understand any reassignment of the hero of Gettysburg unless Meade requested it. If Lincoln made a change, he felt it would be seen a reflection upon General Meade who, in the eyes of the public, had done nothing to warrant such action. (12)

Smith went to New York on leave before the campaign began. Grant called him back to Washington and the two went to Fortress Monroe to visit General Butler. (13) Grant then assigned Smith to the Army of the James and his orders, dated April 19, 1864, read that he was assigned, "to duty as of that date [March 31, 1864] under the orders of General Butler." (14) Grant's instructions to Smith were that he was leaving General Butler in command of the Army of the James, and Smith would have a corps under Butler. Smith was, "to keep him [Butler] straight in military matters." (15) Smith contacted Colonel Babcock of Grant's staff on April 26 trying to get clarification of Grant's intentions. Babcock wrote back on April 29 "the general is very fixed in letting Butler have his own way with all minutiae." (16) Smith called his instructions "untruthful" (dishonest). (17) Another word would have been "impossible."

Butler had an ego that was limitless. He considered himself a military expert, he despised most West Pointers, and he had tremendous political influence. General Smith was expected to control Butler's military actions but he was powerless for he was given no authority to do so. Butler was so important politically in the Fall 1864 presidential campaign that only President Lincoln could have dealt with him. If General Smith attempted to carry out Grant's instructions, he was certain to lose for he would not be supported in his efforts.

Butler's military career started as a third lieutenant in the Massachusetts militia, in 1840. As a member of the Lowell Guard for three years he learned the duties of a soldier. In 1855 he was promoted to brigadier general in the militia. For four years, he encamped with his brigade, 1857-1860. (18) These ranks were associated with his political positions in Massachusetts and were not based upon military training and experience. (19) Butler was a Massachusetts Democrat who served in the state's House of Representatives and Senate. He served as a delegate to the Democratic National Convention (1848-1860). His relationship with West Point and West Pointers ranged from positive to strongly negative. Butler, a newly minted brigadier general in the militia, was appointed by President Franklin Pierce as a visitor at West Point for the purpose of examining that institution. (20) As a young man, Benjamin Butler considered applying for an appointment to the U.S. Military Academy at West Point and then gave up the idea. As a congressman, he appointed his son, Ben Israel to the Academy. Ben graduated, served one year, and never served again. His daughter, Blanche, married Adelbert Ames (West Point 1861) who became a distinguished Union general. (21) His grandson, Butler Ames attended the Academy after the Civil War. (22) All of these appear to be on the plus side. However, his autobiography, *Butler's Book*, is filled with criticisms of West Point and West Pointers.

At the start of the Civil War, General Butler thought the Confederates had an excellent opportunity to capture Washington. When Jefferson Davis (West Point 1828) didn't cease Washington Butler said the problem was "his training at West Point where the necessity of a rapid movement in war-time operations was taught in the negative." (23) He went on to say "that sort of instruction, as we shall see as we go on, caused several direful results in the movements of both armies . . ." (24)

In April, 1861, General Butler landed his troops at Annapolis, Maryland. The New York Seventh Regiment under the command of Colonel Lefferts was already there. As the senior officer, Butler gave Lefferts an order. A civilian, who claimed that he was trained at West Point, and traveled with Lefferts, told Butler that he had no authority to issue an order to troops of another state. Colonel Lefferts followed that advice and refused to obey Butler's order. Shortly after, the officers of the New York regiment met and agreed to march to Washington with the Eighth Massachusetts. Butler had outmaneuvered the colonel. The movement secured Washington. (25). President Lincoln was grateful and appointed Benjamin Butler as a major general in the U.S. Volunteers, ranking from May 16, 1861. (26)

Shortly after that incident, Lt. Col. Erasmus Keyes arrived in Annapolis. He was on the staff of General-in-Chief Winfield Scott. Keyes said he found no "regular" officer in command, and decided that it was his duty to take charge. As a lieutenant colonel in the regular army he proceeded to give orders to militia general Butler. Butler sent Colonel Hamilton to see General Scott, and Hamilton returned with Scott's order dated April 27, 1861, assigning command of the new Department of Annapolis to General Butler. (27) Butler wrote in his book, "So I was again out of the shadow of West Point." (28) He used his influence to get his way.

General Butler's influence reached far beyond his native state. He relates three incidents in his autobiography citing his command in national politics.

The year 1864 was a year involving a presidential election. Lincoln was striving to be reelected; Secretary of the Treasury Salmon Chase was vying to replace him as the Republican candidate. In early spring, an official of the Treasury Department approached General Butler and offered the candidacy for the position of vice president on the Chase ticket. Butler refused the offer. (29)

Within three weeks of that offer, former Secretary of War Simon Cameron met with General Butler as President Lincoln's representative. He indicated that the current vice president, Hannibal Hamlin, would be replaced on the Lincoln ticket and offered General Butler the opportunity to take his place. Butler also turned down his offer. (30)

After Lincoln won reelection, Cameron again visited General Butler as Lincoln's representative. This time he offered Butler the position of Secretary of War replacing Stanton. Again, Butler refused the offer saying he preferred to remain in the military in a command position. (31)

Butler's first military action in the Civil War was the Battle of Big Bethel on June 10, 1861. It was a humiliating Union defeat. The next action was a combined Army-Navy attack upon Fort Hatteras on August 27-28 1861.The attack was a success, primarily due to the Navy's bombardment. From there, all of Butler's military actions resulted in failure, whether it was action he planned or the plans of others he interfered with, or plans of others that he rejected. The most egregious of these was Bermuda Hundred in May 1864.

While Benjamin Butler did not recognize his own deficiencies in carrying out military operations, others did. On April19, 1864, Confederate General Robert E. Lee wrote to President Jefferson Davis, ". . . . General W. F. Smith has been ordered to command the troops around Fortress Monroe. . . . . If the latter [an operation starting from Fortress Monroe] is true, would indicate that actions are contemplated from that quarter which they did not wish to trust to General Butler." (32)

CHAPTER 22

The Army of the James
March 31-May 16, 1864

As indicated earlier, Generals Grant and Smith went to see General Butler at Fortress Monroe on April 1, 1864. Grant gave Butler written instructions on April 2. Butler's objective was Richmond. He was to assemble 20,000 men from his own command which would be supplemented with 10,000 more from the Department of the South under General Quincy Gilmore (West Point 1849). (1) The instructions read, "Maj. Gen. W. F. Smith is ordered to report to you, to command the troops sent into the field from your department." (2) If Grant intended to limit Butler's authority to conduct military operations as Smith understood, he didn't forbid Butler from drawing up plans of operation or giving orders to commanders in the field during operations. Therein lay the problem.

Smith did not participate in the discussions between Grant and Butler on April 1 and 2. After General Grant left Fortress Monroe, General Butler took Smith to his office and showed Smith his plan of operations which Butler said Grant had approved. Smith said he was "astounded" for he felt that the plan was faulty and could hardly believe that Grant had approved it. After further discussion with Butler, Smith suggested a different movement which was in accord with Grant's earlier proposal to Halleck in the winter of 1863-64, one prepared by Smith. That proposal was based on striking the Confederate communications below Richmond, using a base in the Carolinas. (3)

Butler sent Smith to see Grant on April 15 to advocate again his plan. (4) Grant soundly rejected the proposal. He said his mind was made up and he expected Butler to concentrate his forces, seize

City Point, ". . . . and act from there, looking upon Richmond as your objective point." (5)

Grant's plan was to have 23,000 men from Butler's command take to the field under General Smith. As noted this force was be supplemented by 10,000 men from the forces of the Department of the South under General Gilmore. (6) General Halleck wrote General Gilmore on April 4, 1864 ordering the movement of his forces. (7) No deadline was given. Gilmore wrote to Butler on April 16, indicating he had organized the Tenth Corps into three brigades. Significantly, he said," Great delay has occurred here in concentrating my scattered forces, but it could not have been avoided." He also said, "I do not propose to leave here [Hilton Head, South Carolina] until my troops are in motion and the last regiment ready to embark." (8)

On April 23 Butler wrote to his fellow Bay-Stater, Senator Henry Wilson, head of the Senate Committee on Military Affairs, "Please have no action taken at present on General Gilmore's confirmation if he is likely to be rejected. His corps is ordered here and I should not like to change commanders just now." (9)

General Grant expected General Butler to move his forces towards Richmond on May 4. (10) General Gilmore arrived at Fortress Monroe that day; the Eighteenth Corps under Smith and the Tenth Corps under Gilmore embarked on May 4 as planned. The transports sailed up the James River and the troops disembarked on May 6 at Bermuda Hundred. They were unopposed. (11)

Then Butler wrote Senator Wilson again on May 7 asking Wilson to bring Gilmore's name before the Senate and have him rejected. He wrote, ". . . he is wholly useless in the movement of troops." (12) Attorney Butler started building a case against Quincy Gilmore. Smith's turn would come later.

Ignoring Grant's directions that Smith would command the troops in the field, General Butler directed operations at Bermuda Hundred. He had drawn up a plan without any engineering help, no reconnaissance, and no understanding of the topography. On May 8 Butler ordered Smith with his Eighteenth Corps and Gilmore with his Tenth Corps to attack. In his order to Gilmore, he wrote, "The enemy are in our front with cavalry, 5,000 men and it is a disgrace that we are cooped up here." (13)

On May 9, Smith and Gilmore were ordered to demonstrate against Petersburg and ran into unexpected obstacles. Swift Creek, which lay between the Bermuda Hundred and Petersburg, was impossible to cross and the two bridges across it were well fortified. Jointly, they wrote to Butler suggesting an alternate approach by quickly building a bridge over the Appomattox River. Both men were superb engineers. Butler rejected their proposal and, according to Smith, said to his staff that "he did not propose to build a bridge for the West Point men to retreat across." Smith wrote "To such a smear there was no answer but it must have had a tendency to make the relations more rigidly official and to check any disposition on the part of General Gilmore and myself to volunteer any advice." (14) (15)

On May 12 Butler ordered Smith and Gilmore to attack again, this time toward Richmond. On May 14 Smith and Brooks made a reconnaissance of the Rebel works in front of them and felt they could be carried. Smith sent Lieutenant Michie with a written report of the situation to General Butler and said he would attack if Butler ordered it. Butler fumed that Smith was trying to put the responsibility on him. General Smith wrote that, "There came no order and though it satisfied me that I had correctly estimated the character of the general commanding, I reported that the assault was not made and that the general had not come to my position and have[sic] asked my advice about the matter." (16) (17)

Smith expected too much of General Butler, for as General Isaac Wistar wrote after the war, "If General Butler made any personal examination at all of his army's fighting line on that occasion, [in front of Drewry's Bluff] it was unknown to us, for although holding an important command in that action and personally present on the line of battle, I did not at any time see the commanding general there, or hear of his presence within two miles of it." (18)

At Drewry's Bluff, Smith made a personal reconnaissance and concluded that the Rebel fortifications were too strong to be attacked. Then, on May 16, Pierre G.T. Beauregard (West Point 1838) attacked General Heckman's portion of the line, captured Heckman and crushed his Star Brigade. The Union movement failed and the troops returned to their entrenchments. (19) General Grant described Butler's position as having a strong defensive line of entrenchments across the neck of Bermuda Hundred and facing an equally strong line held by the Confederates. It was if Butler was in a bottle and the enemy had corked the bottle. (20)

CHAPTER 23

Joining the Army of the Potomac
May 17-June 1, 1864

After Butler's failed attempt to move toward Richmond, General Smith wrote to General Grant. He said that the interests of the country would be better served by withdrawing Butler's force within his strong lines, leaving him sufficient force to defend himself and sending the remainder of the command to reinforce the Army of the Potomac. (1) Grant's reaction, on May 21, was to direct Halleck to determine what prevented the "effective use" of Butler's command. Grant said that the problem might be Butler or his subordinates, Smith and Gilmore, and noted that Smith was obstinate and condemned any proposal that he did not suggest. (2)

That same day, General Halleck gave the assignment to Brigadier General M.C. Meigs, (West Point 1836), Quartermaster of the Army and Brigadier General J.G. Barnard (West Point 1833), Chief Engineer of the Armies in the Field. Their initial report, made on May 23, stated, "We have not been able fully to post ourselves as to the relations of the corps commanders, but think the report of want of harmony may be exaggerated, at least so far as General Smith is concerned." (3)

Their full report is dated May 24. They said "What in our opinion ought to be done, is, either, first, to place an officer of military experience and knowledge in command of these two corps, thus making them a unit for field operations, and then assume the offensive, or second, to withdraw 20,000 men to be used elsewhere . . . . General Butler is satisfied with the aid and ability of General William F Smith. He does not appear to be satisfied with General Gilmore. General Butler evidently desires to retain command in the field. If his desires must be gratified, withdraw Gilmore, place Smith in command of both corps under the supreme command of General Butler . . . . success would be more certain were Smith in command untrammeled and General Butler remanded to the administrative duties of the department." (4)

In an exchange between Grant and Halleck on May 24, Halleck reported that he had prepared orders to General Smith to join Grant with 20,000 men. Grant said he had reports that Lee was retreating to Richmond and Smith might be needed where he was and Butler was to hold Smith in readiness to move and to await further orders, (5) Later on May 24 Halleck ordered Butler to have 20,000 men ready to be moved. (6) On May 25 Grant ordered Halleck to send the troops from Butler's force "to White House to land on the north side and march to join this army." (7) Halleck sent the orders on May 26, and directed that Smith lead the column. (8) Butler reported the next day that he was sending Smith to White House with 17,000 infantry, and some cavalry and artillery, about 20,000 in all. (9) Smith requested permission to land at West Point rather than White House. He felt the change would save time. (10) No action was taken on his request. It turned out that Smith had been correct for Colonel Esposito wrote in the West Point Atlas of the Civil War, "Smith reached White House only to find no facilities for disembarking his troops . . . ."(11)

Both Generals Butler and Smith knew that Smith was to lead troops to join the Army of the Potomac. Despite that, at 2:30 P.M. on May 28, Butler ordered Smith to take his column of troops and attack Petersburg. If Smith complied, it would have meant disobeying Grant's orders and not joining the Army of the Potomac. Smith responded by requesting "that the orders for the movement of tomorrow, for my command, may be furnished to me to-night in writing" They were not and Butler was forced to send Smith and his column to Grant. (12)

On May 28, a bitter General Butler ordered Smith to embark. His orders read, in part, ". . . . .in consequence of imperative orders from General Grant your column will move to his assistance . . . . I grieve much that this weakness of the Army of the Potomac has called the troops away, just as we were taking the offensive, and that the attack on Petersburg, which was agreed on to take place tomorrow morning, must be abandoned." (13)

That same day General Butler appealed to Secretary Stanton. He wrote, in part," . . . I found that the rebels had uncovered Petersburg, and its importance as a depot to them cannot be overrated. I had proposed to attack the place to-morrow morning, with every prospect of success, but the imperative orders transmitted through General Halleck, and the arrival of the transportation, although not sufficient in my judgment, but yet sufficient to begin with, rendered necessary a change of order . . . . I regret exceedingly the loss of the opportunity upon Petersburg." (14)

In the course of all this activity, Grant and Halleck were considering recommending promotions to the ranks of major general and brigadier general in the regular army. Meade and Sherman were being considered for major general and Hancock for brigadier general. Halleck wrote Grant on May 23, "Perhaps you will be enlightened a little by knowing what are some of the outside influences. I understand the names of Butler and Sickles have been strongly urged by politicians, in order, as they say to break down 'the West Point' influence." It will not be difficult to draw conclusions, This is *entre nous*." (15) The withdrawal of Smith's column and the abandonment of the proposed attack denied Butler an opportunity to gain fame.

On May 28, General Smith contacted Admiral Lee for help in guarding the transportation of the troops by water. Admiral Lee responded, "Your message tonight is the first official notice I had of your movement." (16) At 1:10 A.M. on May 29 Baldy Smith wired General Halleck that the vanguard of his column under General Ames would leave Bermuda Hundred for White House at daylight on May 30. (17)

Also on May 28, Brigadier General John Rawlins, Grant's chief of staff, wired Smith that after he landed at White House, he was to move to New Castle on the Pamunkey and there await further orders. (18) Colonel Esposito wrote, ". . . the frustrated Smith had finally disembarked his command at White House by 3:00 P.M. on the 31, and had marched without waiting for all his wagons and reserve ammunition to be gotten ashore. His march, however, promptly became a wild goose chase, either Grant himself or Maj. Gen. John A. Rawlins, the chief of Grant's personal staff, twice made idiotic errors in Smith's orders, sending him north to the Pamunkey instead of west to Old Cold Harbor." (19)

General Grant issued orders on May 30, assigning Smith to General Meade's command. (20) However, for a brief period Smith communicated directly with Grant. He attempted to get instructions from Grant as to whether he should wait at White House until his supplies and ammunition were unloaded or march to New Castle without waiting. Grant sent him a reply but it did not reach Smith. That response was for Smith to wait and receive his supplies before marching. (21)

General Smith had landed most of his troops by 3:00 P.M. on May 31. He marched toward New Castle, as directed, halting just short of that place by 11:00 P.M. His troops suffered from the heat and hard marching. (22) (23) When Smith reached New Castle he found no one there. Then a staff officer sent by Grant, Lieutenant Col. Orville Babcock, arrived with the correct instructions. (24) (25) He immediately started for Cold Harbor ". . . . .having been by this blunder led out of my way about ten miles." (26)

When Smith's aide reported to General Meade and explained that Smith had hurried to carry out his orders and had inadequate supplies of ammunition with him for an attack, Meade exploded and said, "Why the Hell didn't he wait for his supplies to come up before coming here?" (27) It wasn't a very auspicious start of the relationship between Smith and his Eighteenth Corps and Meade and the Army of the Potomac.

CHAPTER 24

The Battle of Cold Harbor
June 1-3, 1864

The Battle of Cold Harbor was a disaster for the Army of the Potomac. Serious mistakes were made by both Grant and Meade. Smith and his Eighteenth Corps paid dearly for them. The needless loss of men made an indelible impression on Baldy Smith, one which would later color his actions in the first attack on Petersburg.

Lieutenant General U. S. Grant had decided to make his headquarters in the field with the Army of the Potomac. While there were advantages to this arrangement, its weakness was that the army had two heads and sometimes communications broke down. This happened at Cold Harbor.

Grant's first orders to Smith sent the Eighteenth Corps to New Castle. With corrected orders, Smith left New Castle and marched to Cold Harbor. He was hampered by reduced numbers and the lack of supplies and ammunition. General Smith had left City Point with 16,000 infantry. (1) Under Rawlins' order, he was required to leave a garrison at White House until it was relieved. He left General Ames' division of 2,500 men. (2) General John J. Abercrombie (West Point 1822) was scheduled to relieve Ames so that Ames could rejoin the Eighteenth Corps. Upon his arrival at White House, Abercrombie directed Ames to remain until he decided to relieve him. (3) Finally, on June 3 after General Smith appealed to General Grant, Ames was released and joined Smith but his arrival was too late to help Smith when he needed him most. (4)

On June 1 General Meade ordered General Smith to follow General Horatio Wright, (West Point 1841) and his Sixth Corps, take a position on the Sixth Corps' right, hold the road from Cold Harbor to Bethesda Church and join Wright in his attack. (5) The line Smith was to hold was over three miles long. He felt that he could not hold the line and attack at the same time and decided to join Wright in his assault. General Wright waited long enough for Smith to make a hasty inspection of the enemy's lines and prepare his line of battle before he started. (6)

Smith's infantry was short on ammunition as all the men had was what they carried on their persons. (7) The Eighteenth Corps assaulted the enemy lines at 4:30 P.M. that day without an adequate supply of bullets and didn't receive a fresh supply until the Sixth Corps was able to provide it around 7:00 A.M. on June 2. (8)

Smith's three divisions, General Charles Devens', General James Rickett's (West Point 1839) and General John Martindale's (West Point 1835) assaulted the Rebel lines and carried them at all points. The Confederate defenses were so cleverly constructed that General U. S. Grant reported that the positions carried were untenable and had to be given up. (9) Smith wrote about the battle of June 1, 1864, "In this fight, I found that my right flank was 'in the air' and to protect it from being turned, I was obliged to reform it. This gave the enemy a chance to pour in a very destructive enfilading fire on the troops engaged in the assault which accounts for my serious losses." (10) The Eighteenth Corps lost 448 killed, 2,365wounded, and 206 missing or captured for a total of 3,019. After the battle on June 1 Smith reported to Meade that his strength was barely 9,000 men. He also reported that his line was very thin, his men were low on ammunition, and that he was in such a condition in which he might not be able to hold the line if vigorously attacked.(11)

At 10:45 P.M., General Meade proposed to General Grant that they attack early on the morning of June 2. He said "I have heard nothing from Smith, and do not believe he was much engaged this afternoon." (12) At 1:30 A.M. on June 2, Smith reported to Meade that he felt that his line was "perfectly indefensible" without additional troops. (13) When Smith received Meade's order to attack in the morning, he sent a dispatch back stating that he had tried to represent his condition and added, "In the present condition of my line an attack by me would be simply preposterous." (14) The time for the attack was changed to early evening. Then General Grant ordered that the attack time be changed again. He wrote to Meade, "General: In view of the want of preparation for an attack this evening, and the heat and want of energy among the men from moving during the night last night, I think it advisable to postpone assault until early tomorrow morning." (15)

In the meantime, General Smith was having trouble getting artillery ammunition. He sent for ammunition from General Henry Hunt (West Point 1839), Chief of Artillery, only to be told that he was extravagant with his use of ammunition and was given some but with limits put on it. (16) When Meade learned of Hunt's action, he told Smith he would be given all the ammunition and artillery he needed and he should ignore Hunt's strictures. (17)

Baldy Smith also encountered problems in getting his own ammunition and supplies unloaded at White House. On June 3, Smith reported to General Rufus Ingalls (West Point 1843), Chief Quartermaster of the Army of the Potomac, that his quartermaster had been delayed because the docks that he had using had been taken from him. (19) The result was that he could not send Smith's ammunition to him in a timely manner. Finally, General Grant corrected the problem by issuing Special Order No. 24 on June 4 placing General Meade in command of the movement of supplies to the Army of the Potomac "without reference to the territorial department in which they may be or to which they belong . . . ." (20) The top general in the Union army had to settle a minor bureaucratic problem.

General Meade and General Smith exchanged, sometimes heated, communications in which Meade expected Smith to attack and Smith tried to portray his situation. When General Smith received the order to attack at 4:30 A.M. on June 3, he was "exceedingly shocked." (21) Both General Grant and General Meade knew that the Confederate defenses at Cold Harbor were virtually impregnable. They also knew, as General Humphreys wrote in his authoritative book on the Virginia Campaign, that a well defended force had an advantage of more than four to one over an attacking force. (22) The only hope for success was to attack at weak points in the Rebel lines with overwhelming force. The decision to assault the Confederate's fortified positions across the entire line on June 3 ceded all the advantages to the Confederates.

From Smith's point of view the attacks on June 3 started badly and stayed that way throughout the day. There was a gap in the line on his right, and he contacted General Wright saying that he would conform to Wright's advance "so that the two corps might be working in unison."

Wright responded that, "he was going to pitch in." According to General Smith that left him no choice but to carry out Meade's order literally and he wrote "precisely at 4:30 A.M. I gave the murderous order." (23)

The alignment of the Army's corps at Cold Harbor on June 3 was, from left to right, Hancock's Second Corps, Wright's Sixth Corps, and Smith's Eighteenth Corps. Further to the right was Warren's Fifth Corps, and still further to the right was Burnside Ninth Corps. The first assault was made at the designated time by Hancock, Wright, and Smith. (24) General Humphreys wrote, "The greater part of the fighting was over in an hour or less." (25)

General Smith made his main attack through a ravine in the center of his line. There Stannard's brigade of Martindale's division made three gallant assaults but was repulsed. Stannard's losses were 31 commissioned officers and 462 enlisted men. (26)

Colonel Esposito wrote in the West Point Atlas of the Civil War, "At 4:30 AM. 3 June, the II, VI, and XVIII advanced. In less than an hour, their assault collapsed with 7,000 casualties. (the Confederates lost 1,500). Neither Meade nor Grant had taken the precaution of reconnoitering Lee's lines or had paid particular attention to organizing the attack." (27)

At 7:00 A.M., U. S. Grant sent the following message to General Meade, "The moment it becomes certain that the assault cannot succeed, suspend the offensive . . ."(28) Despite this admonition, Meade continued to order attacks.

Corps commanders started sending in reports that they could not advance unless the corps on their flank also advanced. At 7: 45 A.M., General Wright reported that he was in advance of everyone else and that he could not advance further without a corresponding advance by Smith. Then, with a somewhat snide comment, he added, "I may be pardoned for suggesting that the important attack for our success is by the Eighteenth Corps." (29)

By 8:00 A.M., General Smith reported that his troops were very much used up and that he had no hope of being able to carry the works in front of him unless the Sixth Corps could relieve him from the galling fire on his left flank. (30) General Meade then told both Wright and Smith to assault without reference to the other. (31) The pattern continued. At 8:45 A.M., General Hancock reported that he considered the attack a failure but would try again if any of the other corps had any success. (32)

Warren proposed a coordinated attack, and Meade responded at 8:45 A.M., "that you must not wait for simultaneous attacks, but push forward your assaults." (33) And at 10:00 A.M. Warren was told that Smith was attacking, was hard pressed, and that he was expected to relieve the pressure on Smith. (34)

Actually, when General Smith received the last order to attack, he refused to obey. He wrote," I was willing to take myself all the consequences of my action, but I was not willing to assent to the sacrifice of any more troops. General Meade informed General Grant who sent his Chief Engineer, Colonel Comstock, to go over my front . . . . I knew of course that I was on trial, but as I never heard anything more of the matter. I concluded that Comstock had found I had sufficient reasons for doing what is generally unwarrantable on the field of battle. It was a terrible responsibility for a subordinate to take but I had what seemed to me a greater responsibility on the other hand. The lives of the soldiers were intrusted to me with the command of them and were not to be wasted uselessly." (35)

Finally, at 12:30 P.M., General Grant sent this message to General Meade, "The opinion of corps commanders not being sanguine of success in case an assault is ordered, you may direct a suspension of farther advance at the present." (36) At 1:00 P.M. on June 3, General Meade ordered the suspension of further offensive operations and the entrenchment of the positions the corps held. (37) In his memoirs, General Grant wrote," I have always regretted that the last assault at Cold Harbor was ever made. . . . . At Cold Harbor no advantage whatever was gained to compensate for the heavy loss we sustained." (38)

General Meade's reaction was quite different. The arrangement of having two leaders for the Army of the Potomac was taking its toll. On May 30 Meade wrote his wife," The papers are giving Grant all the credit of what they call success. I hope they will remember this if anything goes wrong."(39) "I feel a satisfaction in knowing that my record is clear, and that the results of this campaign are the clearest indications I could wish of my sound judgment, both at Williamsport and Mine Run. In every instance that we have attacked the enemy in an entrenched position we have failed . . . . So, likewise whenever the enemy has attacked us in position, he has been repulsed." (40) After the attacks on the 3 of June, General Meade visited Smith's headquarters. From their conversation, Smith concluded that the lack of a plan at Cold Harbor was due to jealousy on Meade's part. Meade said that, ". . . . .if Grant was commanding the army he might furnish the plan." (41) General Smith never forgave General Meade for the attacks at Cold Harbor.

CHAPTER 25

The Attack at Petersburg
June 14-15, 1864
(Until 5:00 P.M. June 15)

The attack at Petersburg on June 15, 1864 involved a breakdown in communications between Grant and Meade, Hancock being delayed by Butler and given a faulty map, and an impetuous, incompetent general, Butler, taking the lead. General Smith was caught in the middle of this mess and his critics succeeded in using his actions at Petersburg to sully his name.

Following the debacle at Cold Harbor Grant decided to move his army across the James River and attack Richmond from the rear via Petersburg. General Grant revealed his plans for the Eighteenth Corps on June 11 when he sent General Meade this message, "The movement will be made as heretofore agreed upon . . . . that is, the Eighteenth Corps make a rapid march with the infantry alone, their wagons and artillery accompanying the balance of the army to Cole's Landing or Ferry [later changed to White House] and there embark for City Point [changed to Bermuda Hundred], losing no time for rest until they reach the latter point."(1) The Eighteenth Corps was singled out for a special assignment, but Smith was not told what it was.

The specifics of Grant's plan for capturing Petersburg were unknown to Meade's Chief of Staff, General Humphreys. How much General Meade knew is a matter of conjecture. Humphreys wrote in his book:

> "It appears that General Grant's plan for capturing Petersburg was something like the following, though I am

without positive information on the subject. The force holding the town was known to General Butler to be very small, merely the artillery of the works, Wise's Brigade, 2,400, with some local militia to be called from their daily vocations at need, and Dearing's cavalry, 2,000. (2)

With the return of Smith's Command, General Butler would have 23,000 or 24,000 infantry, and with 3,000 cavalry and 14,000 infantry, with due proportion of artillery, sent with Smith against Petersburg early in the day, and with 10,000 infantry and sufficient artillery at the Bermuda Hundred lines, the capture of Petersburg seemed to be certain. The undertaking might very properly be considered to belong to Butler's command, and apparently it was designed that the Second Corps and such of the troops of the Army of the Potomac as might need to follow should not take part in the capture, which was amply provided for, but go into position of support . . . ."(3)

General Grant sent his orders to General Butler on June 11. He advised Butler that Smith had 15,000 men and that he would join Butler without wagons or artillery. "Expecting the arrival of the Eighteenth Corps by Monday night, if you deem it practicable from the force you now have to seize and hold Petersburg, you may prepare to start on arrival of troops to hold your present lines. I do not want Petersburg visited, however, unless it is held, nor an attempt to take it unless you feel a reasonable degree of confidence of success." (4) (Underlining supplied)

General Butler wrote in his book, "General Grant had instructed me that if I thought Petersburg could be captured, I should send that corps [the Eighteenth] under command of Smith in the morning with such force as I could spare to make the attack." (5) Butler's assertion was not consistent with Grant's written orders.

U.S. Grant was noted for the clarity of his communications. His orders were ". . . . if you deem it practicable from the force you now have [Gilmore's Tenth Corps, Kautz's Cavalry, and Hinks' Colored Division] to seize and hold Petersburg, you may start on arrival of troops [the Eighteenth Corps] to hold your present lines."

On June 14, General Grant traveled to Bermuda Hundred and met with General Butler to direct the movement for the attack. (6) That same day, Butler relieved Gilmore from command. If Butler made the attack he had to have someone else to lead it.

Earlier, General Butler had attempted to capture Petersburg on June 9 and it had been a dismal failure. He had sent General Quincy Gilmore to attack the Confederate defenses there. The attacking force consisted of General Kautz (West Point 1852) with 1,800 cavalry, General Hinks with 1,200 or 1,300 colored troops, and Colonel Hawley with another 1,500 infantry.(7) The total force numbered between 4,500 and 4,600. The only written orders Butler gave to Gilmore were "This is not to be artillery work, but a quick decisive rush." General Gilmore reported that General Hincks faced artillery and reinforced infantry and said that it would be impossible to carry the defenses in front of him by assault. In Colonel Hawley's front, the enemy fought outside his works and it became evident to Colonel Hawley and he so reported that an assault would fail. (8) General Kautz reported on June 11 that he was stopped by artillery and infantry, and hearing nothing from General Gilmore, he returned to Bermuda Hundred. (9) In his report, Kautz indicated that he suffered 36 casualties, had lost one piece of artillery and two carriages, and had captured 42 Rebels.

General Butler refused to accept Gilmore's report although he had not been near the front during the expedition. Butler was convinced that Beauregard had no more than 2,000 defenders and that the city could easily be captured. (10) He used Gilmore's report as an excuse to get rid of Gilmore, a general he did not want.

Lt. Col. Comstock, Grant's respected Aide-de-Camp was at Butler's headquarters when General Gilmore returned from his attack. Comstock wired General Grant "Gilmore reconnoitered the enemy's works and found them strong." (11) This was the first indication that the Rebel defenses were stronger than Butler had portrayed them. General Smith and his Eighteenth Corps were being sent to attack positions of unknown strength and they were exhausted from fighting and marching. They were not in good condition to take on another battle.

General Smith described the status of his command after the Battle of Cold Harbor in a letter to Grant's Chief of Staff Rawlins dated June 9, 1864, "I find it impossible to detail officers of my command, the officers most suitable to fill staff appointments, on account of the fearful loss of field officers from the late engagements. I started from General Butler's command with five brigades of this corps and four of the Tenth Corps. I have since consolidated the whole force into three divisions of the Eighteenth Corps. I respectfully ask that the status of this command be settled now, and that I be allowed either to appoint or send forward names to fill the corps staff, or that the names I send in may be detailed temporarily with me." (12)

Baldy Smith received first knowledge that the Eighteenth Corps was to move and cross the James River was when John Rawlins, Grant's chief of staff, directed him on June 13 to return to Bermuda Hundred as fast as possible. No explanation was given for the move. (13)

In the meantime, General Butler was organizing the force to be given Smith. On June 14, he told General Hinks that his division of colored troop was to join General Smith before daybreak on June 15 (14) On the 14 Butler told General Terry, Acting Commander of the Tenth Corps, that he was sending Kautz and 3,000 cavalry to join Smith. In the process, Butler indicated that he was holding part of Smith's infantry at Bermuda Hundred as a reserve. (15) General Grant sent a dispatch to General Butler on June 14 "Your attack on Petersburg tonight." (16)

General Smith was worn out from lack of sleep and weak from fever. Upon boarding a steamer at White House on June 13, he slept until the afternoon the next day. The men were equally tired and landed on the June 14, only to be sent into battle the next day.

General Smith and his staff arrived at Butler's headquarters at Bermuda Hundred around sunset on June 14. Butler verbally gave Smith his orders. He had decided to have Smith attack Petersburg at 2:00 A.M. on the June 15. This was complete news to Smith. He had left Cold Harbor with less than 10,000 men. At Bermuda Hundred, Butler gave him Kautz's cavalry and Hincks' division but kept his son-in-laws', Ames', excellent division, at Bermuda Hundred. (17). Smith's force advanced as they disembarked, and he was never quite sure as to how many he had for the attack

Smith asked for an engineer officer to do reconnaissance; Butler refused to give him one. (18) Butler ridiculed any form of reconnaissance and gave the same orders to Smith that he had given to Gilmore on June 9; he was to "rush" ahead. (19) Butler and Kautz assured Smith "that the fortifications at Petersburg amounted to nothing and there was no force of any consequence [there]." (20).

The stage was set for trouble. Smith and his men were exhausted; the intelligence about the Confederate defenses and defenders was wrong; and Grant had failed to tell Meade what he expected the Army of the Potomac to do. (21)

The order of march on the morning of June 15 called for the cavalry to start at 3:00 A.M., following the route it traveled on June 9, where Kautz found "no forces of any consequence" in front of Petersburg. Hinks' Division was to follow the cavalry, and Brook's division was to follow them. Martindale's division took a different route. The cavalry was delayed in starting and the infantry was unable to move until 5:00 A.M. Two hours were lost in the process. About 8:00 A.M., Kautz reported that he had been stopped at a causeway over a swamp by infantry and artillery. This was the officer who had assured Smith that he knew there were few forces in front of Petersburg. General Smith became impatient and ordered the cavalry to retire from the front. General Hinks moved his division forward and captured the position, along with one piece of artillery. They did it handsomely. This was the first fight they had been in and the men were so happy about their success that they behaved like little children. This completely destroyed any semblance of organization, and they, too, had to be withdrawn from the front; in their case to reorganize. (22) (23)

It took Smith some time to get his forces realigned as he wanted them. Another few hours were lost. He was worried about the forces in front of him even though he had been told were "not significant". He wrote, ". . . . the fact that there were troops sufficient in our front to leave the works at Petersburg and come out to meet us induced the belief that that the enemy was much stronger than General Butler supposed and I learned conclusively that our movement was no surprise." (24) General Smith continued, ". . . After the affair at the causeway and the realignment of the forces a march of a mile and a half brought us under fire of the guns in the defenses of Petersburg." (25)

Since he did not have an engineer officer, Smith did his own reconnaissance work. The few positions he found for his guns could not be used for the guns were driven out by the fire of the artillery in the Rebel defenses. (26) One officer described the Confederate defenses as he saw them "There were redoubts connected by breastworks, all of earth and perhaps twenty feet thick at the base and six feet at the top. In front . . . . was a dry ditch perhaps fifteen feet wide and six feet deep, and still [farther] in front of it was the slashing which had been formed by the trees a quarter of a mile in the front." (27) It was a daunting site for the attackers.

Baldy Smith had to find the weak points in the enemy's defenses and then devise a way to attack them. If he did not, Petersburg looked to be a repeat of the murderous attack at Cold Harbor. The reconnaissance must have been agonizing for he wrote, ". . . . and in my physical condition it was a long and painful operation." (28)

Major General William F. "Baldy" Smith

West Point—1831

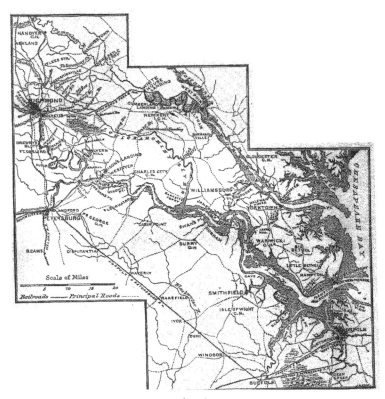

Peninsula of Virginia

Battle of Williamsburg

General Smith and Staff

The Rear Guard at White Oak Swamp

Major General George B. McClellan   Major General William B. Franklin

General Robert E. Lee, CSA

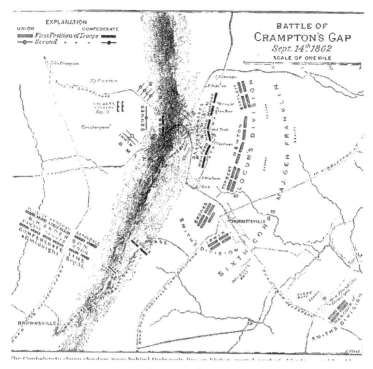

Crampton's Gap

Lincoln and McClellan after Antietam

Major General Ambrose E. Burnside Secretary of War Edwin M. Stanton

Pontoon Bridges over the Rappahannock

Major General Joseph Hooker

Major General Edwin V. Sumner

Fredericksburg, Virginia

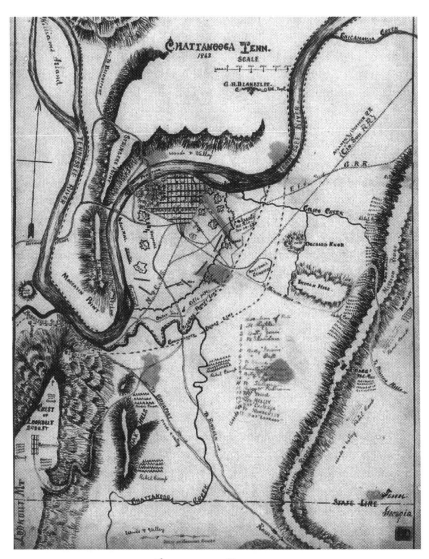

Chattanooga, Tennessee

Lieutenant General U. S. Grant

Major General Benjamin F. Butler and Staff

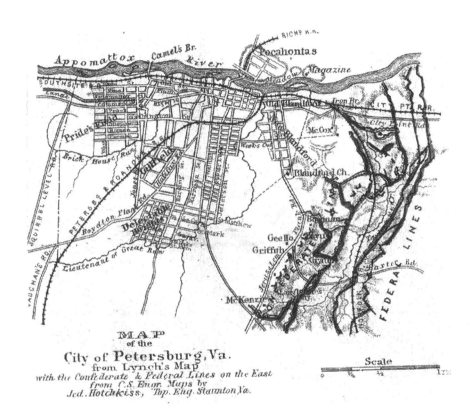

Petersburg, Virginia

Major General George G. Meade   Major General Winfield S. Hancock

18th Corps attacking Petersburg

CHAPTER 26

Petersburg:
The Controversial Phase of the Attack
June 15, 1864

The period from 5:00 P.M. to midnight on June 15 is one of the most controversial periods in the Civil War. No two people who were involved completely agree about events that happened in that time period. General Butler always contended that, "I knew that but a few more troops had been added to Wise's command in Petersburg and all the troops with arms were second class militia, reserves, penitents, and convalescents, did not exceed two thousand effective men." (1) Baldy Smith did not agree. He reasoned that if the enemy could leave his defenses and fight, stopping Kautz's cavalry at the causeway, the Confederates were stronger that Butler and Kautz reported him to be. Smith also stated that he "learned conclusively that the movement was no surprise." (2)

The Confederates started reinforcing the Petersburg defenses on June 14. At that time, Butler's signal officer reported that just before dark he saw two columns, each a half a mile long, approaching the defenses of Petersburg, one from the north and the other from the west. (3) At 1:30 P.M., Smith sent Butler a message, "Have the cars I have heard all day been bringing re-enforcements? There are some Georgia troops in our front." (4) There is no record of Butler responding to that inquiry.

At 4:45 P.M. on June 15, General Grant sent orders to General Meade to send another corps to counter Confederate actions to reinforce their defenses. (5) And at 5:20 P.M. on that day, General Butler sent word to General Grant that two brigades of infantry and 200 wagons and ambulances were crossing Chaffins' farm. (6) Butler's signalman Craft reported at 6:30 P.M. on June 15 that a train of fourteen cars loaded with troops had just passed to Petersburg. He said that the enemy appeared to be sending troops to the defenses on the roads west of the defenses. Then he added that another twenty two cars loaded with troops had also passed going to the fortifications. (7) Despite all the intelligence about Confederate reinforcements, at 7:20 P.M., Butler sent his message to General Smith "I grieve for the delays . . . . Nothing has passed down the railroad to harm you yet." (8) There was no relationship between this dispatch and what was actually happening.

In his report of the action on June 15, Smith wrote "very little infantry could be seen, but that was not proof that it wasn't there, and it was not probable that the number of guns at work against us would be there without strong support." (9) Even though General Smith was not able to determine the strength of the defending force, Lieutenant John Davenport, Butler's aide, claimed that he could. He reported to Butler at 7:00 P.M. on June 15.," I had carefully observed the enemy's line with an eye to the forces which were probably confronting us, and everything seen and unseen, indicated that the information you had in your possession as to their strength—about two thousand men—was correct." (10)

General Humphreys, in his work on the campaign, concluded that the Confederates had an infantry force of 14,000 in the defenses of Petersburg early on June 16. (11) There had been constant movement of reinforcements from June 14 to early on the 16. It was not the static situation that Davenport described.

General Smith needed to find out what he was really facing at Petersburg. He wrote, "During the war, I had made it a rule never to order soldiers into a fight without knowing what was in front of them." (12) This was particularly important to him after the horrible and recent losses at Cold Harbor. As the assault force moved forward at about 11:00 A.M., Kautz and his cavalry were on the extreme left and apart from the main body, Hincks and his troops were on the left, Brooks' division was in the center, and Martindale's division was on the right. (13) The Petersburg entrenchments enclosed the city and were two miles from it. They consisted of strong redans or batteries connected by infantry parapets with high profiles, all with ditches. General Humphrey described Martindale's position "In his front, extending to the Appomattox, was a broad, low valley, cut up by ditches and ravines, completely swept by the enemy's artillery, the intrenchments here being withdrawn some six hundred yards from the salient at and about Jordan's Hill (where the City Point Railroad entered), in front of which was Brooks's division. The line in front of Hinck's division was similarly withdrawn, though not to the same extent. Deep ravines were found along these fronts also. The enemy had a cross-fire of artillery upon the front threatened." (14)

While General Smith was reconnoitering the Rebel defenses, Hancock and his Second Corps were trying to locate a designated position from where they would be able to support the Eighteenth Corps. U.S. Grant had planned to have the Second Corps cross the James River, get 60,000 rations, and march to this designated position near the front. (15) The problem with Grant's plan was that he did not inform Generals Meade, Hancock, or Smith about it. General Butler, who was ordered by Meade to supply the rations, objected to the order claiming Hancock didn't need them. (16) Hancock had to move ahead without the rations, and was angry because he said he had been deceived, and his men did not get anything to eat until the following day. (17) (18)

To compound the problem Army headquarters had given General Hancock a map of the area that was worthless. He was told to go to a designated position on Harrison's Creek that didn't exist. Local inhabitants would not or could not provide any help. Finally, at 5:30 P.M., Hancock's lead division, Birney's, found itself within one mile of Hincks' division of the Eighteenth Corps. (19) Between 5:00 P.M. and 6:00 P.M., Hancock received messages from Generals Grant and Smith indicating that he was expected to support Smith in the attack. This was a complete surprise to General Hancock

General Hincks said, "At about sunset, half-past seven o'clock, I was informed that General Birney in command of two divisions of the Second Corps had halted his column a short distance to the rear of my division and wished to see me." General Hincks knew what General Smith expected the Second Corps to do. General Birney knew nothing of Grant's plan. As a result, when Hincks offered a staff officer to lead Birney's men forward Birney declined the offer. Hincks' proposed another movement of Birney's troops but it was also declined. General

Birney said that he would not move his troops at night in the presence of the enemy over ground with which he was not familiar. (20)

Smith completed his search for weak points in the Confederate defenses around 5:00 P.M. Smith concluded that rather than have the usual assault with massed infantry in close ranks, he" determined to make an attack by throwing forward heavy bodies of skirmishers along my whole line at the same moment, to be supported during the brief period of assault by artillery." (21) Smith carefully explained the plan of attack to General Hincks, Brooks and Martindale. He was ready to move only to find that the artillery horses had been taken for water in an unauthorized move. As a result, it wasn't until 7:00 P.M. when the attack got under way. General Smith wrote, ". . . the success was perfect. In a short time all the works in front of us, including rifle pits, were captured, the division of Brooks taking ten guns, and the division of Hincks' taking six guns. My loss was small, as some of the rebel guns were captured before they were discharged, being loaded with grape to sweep away my assaulting column which they were expecting to advance. It was nearly nine o'clock before the fight was over." (22)

During the attack General Butler, at 7:20 P.M., ordered Smith to "push and get the Appomattox between you and Lee. Nothing has passed down the railroad to harm you yet." (23) At 9:00 P.M., General Smith sent Butler a message, "I must have the Army of the Potomac re-enforcements immediately." (24) Butler's response was received at 9:30 P.M. "Hancock has been ordered up by General Grant's and my orders. Another army corps will reach you by 10:00.A.M. to-morrow. It is crossing. They have not 10,000 men down yet. Push on to the Appomattox." (25)

General Smith reported that about 9 o'clock, General Hancock rode up and asked what he could do. The attack was over. (26) Lt. Col. Morgan, Hancock's chief of staff, wrote that they found that the attack force "had captured a portion of the enemy's line and 17 pieces of artillery . . . . As soon as General Hancock met General Smith he told him that Birney's and Gibbon's divisions, of the Second Corps, were at his service for any place he wished them, stating at the same time that he made the offer of the troops in question for the reason that it was now getting dark and he could not well see the position of the lines, and that General Smith having been on the ground all day knew just what was required to be done. General Smith replied that "all he wished General Hancock to do was to relieve his troops of the Eighteenth corps from their position in the captured works . . . . Both divisions in works at 11:30 P.M. and 12 midnight." (27)

At midnight on July 15, Smith wired Butler," It is impossible for me to go farther to-night; but, unless I misapprehend the topography, I hold the key to Petersburg. General Hancock not yet up." (28)

Footnote: General Smith was so ill the night of June 15, 1864, that he didn't remember that he had received an order from General Butler around 9:00 P.M. to "entrench at once and hold his position." Chapter 31 provides the details about this interesting facet and how, if it had been remembered, might have changed Smith's reputation after the battle.

CHAPTER 27

The Initial Reactions to the Battle of June 15, 1864

As he moved to support the Eighteenth Corps, General Hancock received a message from General Grant. In his report on the action Hancock stated "The same dispatch from Lieutenant General Grant stated that the enemy were throwing re-enforcements into Petersburg and instructed me that should Petersburg not fall on the night of the 15 it would be advisable for General Smith and myself to take up a defensive position and maintain it until all our forces came up. These directions of the lieutenant general were carried out, . . ." (1)

General Smith had asked General Hancock to replace his tired troops who were in the captured works. Hancock reported that by the time this movement was completed, it was too late and too dark for any immediate advance. (2)

At midnight of June 15 Smith had wired Butler, "I hold the key to Petersburg."(3) Assistant Secretary of War Dana agreed. He visited the captured works the morning of June 16 and sent this message to Secretary of War Stanton," The success of Smith last night was of the most important character. He carried these heights, which were defended by works of the most formidable character, and this gives us perfect command of the city and railroad." (4)

General Hancock reported that at 1:00 A.M. on June 16 he gave orders to Generals Birney and Gibbons, whose divisions were up, ". . . that if any commanding points were held by the enemy between their positions and the Appomattox they should be attacked and taken at or before daylight. . . . . These instructions were not promptly complied with, and it was not until about 6 a.m. on the 16 that Generals

Birney and Gibbons advanced to reconnoiter the ground in their front, by which time the enemy had moved a considerable body of fresh troops on the field, had occupied the large redoubts and rifle-pits in front of the Avery house, and had greatly strengthened their positions at all important points." (5)

At 10:30 A.M. on June 16, Grant sent Hancock a dispatch giving him command of all the troops before Petersburg, directing him to push the reconnaissance, and ordering him to prepare for an attack about 6:00 P.M. on that day. Hancock led the Second Corps and two brigades each from the Ninth and Eighteenth Corps in the attack. General Meade described the event in a letter to his wife, "After arriving on the ground, although our men had been marching all the night before and during the day, I at once ordered an attack, which commenced at 6 P.M. and lasted pretty much continuously till 4 A.M. today—that is, ten hours—eight of which were by moonlight, another unparalleled feat in the annals of war." (6)

General Hancock reported, "The advance was spirited and forcible, and resulted, after a fierce conflict, in which our troops suffered heavily, in driving the enemy some distance along our whole line." (7) General Meade summarized the situation, "We find the enemy, as usual, in a very strong position, defended by earthworks, and it looks very much as if we will have to go through a siege of Petersburg, before entering in the siege of Richmond, and that Grant's words of keeping at it all summer will prove to be quite prophetic." (8)

Initially, General Grant was impressed with Smith's accomplishments. He inspected the captured works before General Meade arrived at the front, and wired Meade "General Smith carried very strongly located and well constructed works, forming the left of the enemy's defenses of Petersburg, taking some prisoners and 16 pieces of artillery." (9) Colonel Lyman, of Meade's staff wrote, "On leaving the works with his staff, General Grant met General Meade, and called out 'Well, Smith has taken a line of works stronger than anything we've seen in this campaign'." (10)

In a letter to General Halleck sent on the morning of June 17 U.S. Grant said," Too much credit cannot be given the troops and their commanders for the energy and fortitude displayed during the last five days. Day and night have been all the same, no delays being delayed on any account." (11)

While General Smith was being praised, General Hancock suffered from ill health and was stung by criticism. The wound Hancock received on the third day at Gettysburg caused him to relinquish command of the Second Corps on June 18. General Birney assumed command. (12)

Then, on June 26, Hancock noted he had seen a published telegram from Secretary Stanton which inferred that the reason Petersburg was not captured on June 15 was that the Second Corps did not arrive on time to join Smith. He then saw an article in the New York Times dated June 21 which stated that the attack on June 15 was to have been a joint operation involving the Second Corps and the Eighteenth Corps and the Second Corps did not arrive on time. Hancock called the reports erroneous and prejudicial to him and his command. He wrote," . . . . there appears to be an improper attempt to place the failure to capture Petersburg on the 15 on my command. I respectfully ask for an investigation on this subject." (13)

General Meade forwarded Hancock's request for an investigation to General Grant on June 27. In his forwarding memo, Meade indicated that the events in question happened before he arrived on the field and had he and Hancock been apprised of the contemplated movement, he felt that Hancock could have pushed much earlier to the scene of operations. He continued by noting that actions were occurring he and Hancock did not know about. He ended," . . . I do not see how any censure can be attached to General Hancock and his corps." (14)

General Grant responded to Hancock's request in a memo to General Meade dated June 28. Grant said, "No investigation can now be had without great prejudice to the service, nor do I think an investigation necessary at any time, The reputation of the Second Corps and its commander is so high, both with the public, and in the army, that an investigation could not add to it." Then Grant added, somewhat defensively, "I am very much mistaken if you were not informed of the contemplated movement against Petersburg as soon as I returned to Wilcox's Landing from Bermuda Hundred, and that the object of getting the Second Corps up without waiting for the supply train to come up to issue rations to them, was that they might be on hand if required." (15) (16)

Chapter 28

The Environment of June and July, 1864

As William F. Smith noted in his book published in 1893 "the events that followed Grant's first attack on Petersburg, ... cannot be understood without reference to the exact situation, both political and military at that time." (1) Grant's campaign which encompassed the Wilderness, Spotsylvania, and Cold Harbor resulted in an enormous loss of life and financial resources. Public support in the North for the war was at its lowest point. William Swinton, the noted contemporary war correspondent, wrote "there was at that time great danger of the collapse of the war." (2)

1864 was a presidential election year. The Democrats nominated General McClellan with an appeasement platform. Lincoln was unsure that he would be nominated for a second term and equally uncertain as to his ability to win reelection. He needed all the support he could garner.

General Butler was important politically and incompetent militarily. Grant and Halleck made an attempt to push Butler aside by confining him to his headquarters at Fortress Monroe while Baldy Smith assumed command of all the troops of the department in the field. Butler had a tremendous ego and refused to be pushed aside. He was convinced his qualifications were superior to those of Smith and wrote in his book, *Bulter's Book*, published in 1892 ". . . . It seemed that I had much more experience in moving troops than he had; and as a topographical engineer is not the highest grade at West Point, I did not think I should be insulted by a second grade West Pointer." (3)

Those under Butler had a far different view of his military acumen. General George J. Stannard, a highly respected volunteer from Vermont wrote to his senator, Solomon Foot, "So far as my information extends, the Maj. Genl. Cmdg. this department has not the confidence, to say nothing about the respect, of a single officer or man (leaving out his immediate hirelings) in the whole Department, meaning the 10th & 18th Corps. I have had a good opportunity to learn the feeling that exists in both corps having served in both." (4) General Stannard went on to state that all the officers and men in the command had the utmost confidence in General Smith and ". . . nothing could possibly please them more than to be under his command, untrammeled by any such officer as our present commander." Stannard's entire letter was a plea to Senator Foot asking him to use his influence to rid the Army of the James of General Butler. (5) This was the picture of Butler and the Army of the James after Grant's first attack on Petersburg on June 15, 1864.

On June 16 Butler learned that the Confederates were evacuating their works in his front at Bermuda Hundred. (6) He felt that if he had more troops he could destroy the tracks of the Petersburg railroad. (7) Grant gave him Wright and his Sixth Corps but they were delayed in reaching Bermuda Hundred. (8) Butler was annoyed by Wright's delay and asked for Smith and his Eighteenth Corps, a request Grant refused. (9) After Wright joined Terry and his Tenth Corps they objected to the action Butler proposed. General Butler then sent Wright a message saying, "Do some fighting . . . . I get no fighting but an argument." (10) Wright was hurt and received a lame apology; Terry was demoted from his temporary command of the Tenth Corps and replaced by General Brooks.

Smith and his Eighteenth Corps remained in front of Petersburg for two days after the June 15 attack and then returned to Bermuda Hundred. They were ordered to return to the front on June 21. General Smith issued orders to Stannard to move his First Division at 4:30 A.M., which he did. General Martindale and his Second Division were ordered to move out at 7:30 A.M. (11) Butler saw Martindale moving his troops well after daybreak and assumed that Smith had defied his orders. He fired off this letter to Smith.

June 21, 1864

Major General Smith—To so meritorious and able officer as yourself, and to one toward whom the sincerest personal friendship and the highest respect concur in my mind, I am and ever shall be unwilling to utter a word of complaint; yet I think duty requires that I should call your attention to the fact that your column which was ordered to move at daylight in the cool of the morning is now just passing my headquarters in the heat of the day for a ten-mile march.

The great fault of all movements is dilatoriness, and if this is the fault of your division commanders let them be severely reproved therefore.

I have found it necessary to relieve one general for this among other causes, where it took place in a matter of vital importance, and in justice to him you will hardly expect me to pass in silence a like fault where of less moment. The delay of Grouchy for three hours lost to Napoleon Waterloo and an empire and we all remember the bitterness with which the Emperor exclaimed, as he waited for his tardy general, 'Il s'amuse a Gembloux."

Respectfully,
Benj. F. Butler, Major General Commanding

Smith was furious. He wrote back immediately making no attempt to correct Butler's mistake and refusing to accept Butler's criticism.

Headquarters Eighteenth Army Corps
June 21, 1864, 3:40 P.M.

General,—I have the honor to acknowledge the receipt of your extraordinary note of 9 A.M. In giving your rank and experience all the respect which it is due, I must call your attention to the fact that a reprimand can only come from the sentence of a court-martial, and I shall accept nothing as such. You will also pardon me that I have observing that I have for some years been engaged in marching troops, and I think in experience of that kind, at least, I am your superior. Your accusation of dilatoriness on my part this morning or at any other time since I have been under your orders is not founded in fact, and your threat of relieving me does not frighten me in the least.

Your obedient servant,
W.F. Smith, Major-General

Butler's response was almost immediate. Whether it was sincere or sarcastic and "for the record" is a matter of conjecture.

June 21, 1864, 5:30 P.M.

General Smith,—When a friend writes you a note is it not best to read it twice before you answer unkindly? If you will look at my note you will find it contains no threat. On the contrary, there are some words underlined, that on reading it over it might be possibly so construed.

Please read the note again and see if you cannot wish the reply was not sent. Pardon me for saying in all sincerity that I never thought you at fault as to the movement, as I understood your orders to be as mine were.

Truly you friend;
B.F. Butler

Baldy Smith had had enough; he promptly requested a reassignment. He later wrote in his book "The irritation exhibited in my reply to General Butler may seem excessive, and perhaps it was; but I distrusted General Butler to the last degree." (12)

Headquarters Eighteenth Army Corps
In the Field, Va., June 21, 1864

Brigadier General Rawlins, Chief of Staff of Lieutenant
General Grant:

General:—I have the honor to forward to you copies of
correspondence with General Butler. I have no comments to
make, but would respectfully request that I may be relieved
from duty in the Department of Virginia and North Carolina.
Very respectfully your obedient servant,
W.F. Smith, Major-General (13)

On June 29, General Grant visited Butler's headquarters and
disgraced himself by getting drunk. General Smith said Grant's
inability to handle liquor was well known throughout the army and all
his friends were on guard to keep alcohol away from him. His chief of
staff, Brigadier General John Rawlins, wrote that in March 1863, Grant
pledged to him that he "would drink no more during the war." Then
on June 4, 1863, Rawlins wrote a letter to Grant chastising him for
drinking, reminding him of his pledge, and saying, "Your only salvation
depends upon your strict adherence to that pledge." (14) (15)

General Grant, in his visit to the Army of the James, passed Smith's
headquarters and went with General Butler to Burnside's headquarters.
Burnside always had a selection of alcoholic drinks to entertain his
guests. Grant took at least one drink there. When he and Butler arrived
at Smith's headquarters, he complained of a headache and asked Smith
for a drink. General Smith felt he could not refuse the lieutenant
general's request in Butler's presence and gave him some brandy. When
Grant left, he had to be helped on his horse, his speech was slurred, and
he vomited all over his horse's neck and shoulders. (16)

Upon returning to his tent after General Grant had left, General
Smith said to a staff officer who has witnessed the scene, "General
Grant has gone away drunk. General Butler has seen it, and will never
fail to use the weapon that has been put in his hands." (17)

CHAPTER 29

General Order No. 225

General Grant wrote to General Halleck on July 1 "Mr. Dana, Assistant Secretary of War has just returned. He informs me that he called attention to the necessity of sending General Butler to another field of duty . . . . I have feared that it might become necessary to separate him and General Smith. The latter is really one of the most efficient officers in service, readiest in expedients, and most skillful in the management of the troops in action. I would dislike removing him from his present command unless it was to increase it, but, as I say, may have to do it yet, if General Butler remains." (1) Dana suggested a command for Butler made up of Kentucky, Illinois, and Indiana or one made up of Missouri, Kansas, Illinois, and Indiana. (2)

General Halleck replied to Grant's note on July 3. He said that if Butler was sent to Missouri or Kentucky he would probably cause an insurrection. "Moreover, he would probably greatly embarrass Sherman, if he did not attempt to supersede him, by using against him all his talent at political intrigue, and his facilities for newspaper abuse." (3) Halleck then suggested, "Why not leave General Butler in local command of his department, including North Carolina, Norfolk, Fort Monroe, Yorktown, etc. and make a new army corps of the part of the Eighteenth under Smith?" (4)

On July 6 Grant directed Halleck to prepare the order making the changes he proposed. (5) The order follows.

General Orders No. 225

War Dept. Adj. General's Office
Washington, July 7, 1864

1. The troops of the Department of North Carolina and
    Virginia serving with the Army of the Potomac in the
    field under Major-General Smith will constitute the
    Eighteenth Army Corps, and Maj-Gen. William F. Smith
    is assigned to the command of the corps. Maj.-Gen. B.F.
    Butler will command the remainder of the troops in that
    department, having his headquarters at Fort Monroe.

    By order of the President.

    E.D. Townsend
    Assistant Adjutant General" (7)

The same day the order was prepared, Secretary Stanton sent
General Halleck a note saying that President Lincoln wished to see it
and Grant's correspondence. (7) General Orders No. 225 was issued on
July7 without the phrase "By order of the President". Grant was free to
issue the order but he would have to take full responsibility for it.

General Butler learned of the order on July 9. He and his chief of
staff, Colonel Schaffer, left to see Grant at his headquarters at City
Point. Assistant Secretary of War Dana, who was with Grant when
Butler entered the room, said that Butler, in full uniform and with a
flushed face, held the order in his hand and demanded to know if Grant
issued it. Grant's response was, "No, not in that form." Butler returned
to his camp around dusk, and as he dismounted from his horse, he said
"Gentlemen, the order will be revoked tomorrow." (8) At 6:00 P. M. on
July 9 Butler wired his chief of staff, ". . . . . . Do not trouble yourself
about the order. It is all right now and better than if it had not been
disturbed." He signed the telegram, "Benj. F. Butler Comdg. all the
Troops of the Dept. of Va. and N.C." (9)

General Grant revoked General Orders No. 225 in a letter to General
Halleck, dated July 10, 1864:

"Maj.Gen. H.W. Halleck, Chief of Staff,

General Orders No. 225 of July 7, 1864 would take the Eighteenth corps from the Department of Virginia and North Carolina and leave it a separate command, thus giving a third army in the field. As the Tenth Corps is also serving here, I would not desire this change made, but simply want General Smith assigned to the command of the Eighteenth Corps, and if there is no objection to a brigadier-general holding such a position, General W.T.H. Brooks to the command of the Tenth Corps, leaving both these corps in the department as before, the headquarters of which is at Fortress Monroe. When the Nineteenth Corps arrives, I will add it to the same department. I will take the liberty of suspending the order until I hear again. I will ask to have Gen. Franklin assigned to the active command in the field, under General Butler's orders, as soon as he is fit for duty.

U.S. Grant, Lieutenant General" (10)

In this telegram, General Grant revoked General Orders No. 225, added the Nineteenth Corps to Butler's department and proposed to insert General Franklin between Butler and Smith but with Smith still under Butler's orders. Nothing came of the assignment of General Franklin as Grant had proposed it. Washington viewed Franklin as a "McClellan man" and with the presidential election was less than four months away it did not what to give their opponent's man "another chance to succeed." (11) The rest of the actions were carried out. Butler was retained in command and his department was expanded with the addition of the Nineteenth Corps.

During this period, Baldy Smith suffered ill health and was deeply concerned about the health of his wife who was in Goshen, Vermont. They had lost an infant son and she was suffering from depression. (12) Smith requested leave. Grant wrote a friendly note to Smith on July 2 indicating that he would prefer his not going on leave. He offered sending General Humphreys to help Smith, if necessary. (13) Smith responded to Grant's offer again requesting leave as well as a reassignment. He ended his letter criticizing General Butler. "[I] ask you how you can place a man in command of two army corps, who is as helpless as a child on the field of battle and as visionary as an opium eater in council, and that too, when you have such men as Franklin and Wright available to help you, to make you famous for all time, and our country great and free beyond all other nations of the world." (14) On July 8 General Rawlins notified Smith that his leave was approved. (15)

General Smith went to City Point on July 9 with Franklin who was visiting with his old friends. There they met General Rufus Ingalls, Quartermaster General of the Army of the Potomac and Grant's West Point classmate. Ingalls had a record of furnishing Grant liquor. Franklin wrote "Not long after, Gen. Grant came in and after greeting us; he went to the mantle piece and helped himself to whiskey and water. Shortly afterwards, he took another drink." Smith was "exasperated" with Grant's drinking. (16)

Later that day Smith visited with Grant and unwisely demonstrated one of his damaging traits. He said about himself. "I had a bad habit of saying what I thought and was in hopes that if I were away things might go on more smoothly for some disliked me for my expressed opinions and some were jealous of an influence I was supposed to have at headquarters." (17)

He was furious about Grant's drinking and Ingalls' role in supplying liquor to him but felt he could not talk about it. Instead he vented his anger at Meade's actions at Cold Harbor. Smith recalled "I could not say a word on the subject but I suppose I had to vent my anger on something and I took up the battle of Cold Harbor. There I had been compelled to slaughter some thousands of men and for no good. I could not think on the subject without my eyes filling up. Franklin says I was very severe and I probably was." (18)

At Cold Harbor the Union lost 12,000 while the Confederates lost 2,500. The Eighteenth Corps was in the middle of this Union disaster. After taking severe casualties, Smith refused to execute Meade's order to assault again on June 3. Then Grant's engineer officer, along with other engineers, examined the battlefield and concluded that it would be impossible to storm the Rebel defenses. (19)

Two days later, June 5, General Meade visited Smith's headquarters. Smith asked Meade why there had been no plan for the battle at Cold Harbor. Meade's reply was "that he had worked out every plan for every move from the crossing of the Rapidan onward, that the papers were full of the doings of Grant's army, and that he was tired of it, and was determined to let Grant plan his own battles." (20)

At the end of his tirade on July 9, Smith wrote that Grant "finally acknowledged, to use his own words, that there had been a butchering at Cold Harbor." (21) General Stannard, whose brigade suffered severely at Cold Harbor, was also distressed about Meade's generalship at Cold Harbor. He wrote Senator Foot on July15, 1864, "When I say that this war will be continued to an indefinite time, under our present commanders, I say it in all honesty and wish to include our Lieut. Genl. and especially Genl. Meade, Commanding the Army of the Potomac of whom I used to be proud." (22)

After that General Smith left for Goshen, Vermont to be with his ill wife. (23)

CHAPTER 30

Relieved in Disgrace

Upon his return from Vermont on July 19, General Smith was told that General Grant wanted to see him. The lieutenant general then relieved General Smith and sent him to New York in disgrace.

General Meade wrote his wife on July 20, "Much excitement was created today by the announcement that General W.F. Smith, who returned last evening from his sick leave, was relieved from his command of the Eighteenth Corps and sent to New York. It was only the other day he was assigned by the President to this command, and Butler sent to Fortress Monroe. It appears now the tables are turned—Butler remains and Smith goes." (1)

General Smith was shocked at the turn of events. He started on what would be a life-long pursuit to find out the real reason for his dismissal. At that time, General Grant offered the first of several different reasons he would give for the change. This reason was that "'he could not relieve General Butler and that as I had so severely criticized General Meade, he had determined to relieve me from the command of the 18th Corps and order me to New York City to await orders" (2)

The next morning, Grant gave a different reason for Smith's relief. This one focused on the article in the "Tribune" which had reflected badly on General Hancock efforts in the attack on Petersburg. (3) General Hancock had complained to General Grant about the Tribune article written by a Mr. Kent while he was at Butler's headquarters. Upon receipt of Hancock's complaint, Grant ordered Butler to arrest Kent and send him to Grant's headquarters. Kent left before he could be arrested; Grant then revoked Kent's pass prohibiting him from visiting the army again. (4) Smith was not involved in this incident in any way; the suspicion prevailed that Butler was.

On the morning of July 20, Smith met with Grant again and pressed him for the reason for his removal. Smith recorded "As he was out of reasons for the occasion, he turned on his heel and said 'You talk too much.' This was the last time I ever spoke to him." (5) Smith's good friend and ardent supporter, General James Wilson partially agreed with this reason when he wrote, "His military criticism, however indiscreet, had always been direct and manly." (6)

Later Smith wrote, "Since I have been in New York, I have heard from two different sources (one being from General Grant's headquarters and one a staff officer of a general on intimate relations with General Butler) that General Butler went to General Grant and threatened to expose his intoxication, if the order was not revoked. I also learned that General Butler had threatened to make public something that would prevent the President's re-election. General Grant told me (when I asked him about General Butler's threat of crushing me), that he had heard that General Butler had made some threat with reference to the Chicago convention, which he (Butler) said, he 'had in his breeches pocket' but General Grant was not clear in expressing what the threat was." (7)

General Smith's last contact with General Grant was in a letter dated June 3, 1865. He had heard that Grant had said that the reason for Smith's relief was that he was "getting up a cabal against you [Grant] and was intriguing to get you deposed from your command." Smith wrote to make sure that Grant did not believe the allegation. In his letter, Smith said he was convinced that the only reason he was dismissed was the influence of Butler. He wrote, ". . . . General Martindale assured me that he would make everything right in two hours if I would consent to serve under General Butler as before. To this I replied that I that I had no commission that was worth such a price."

General Cyrus Comstock replied for General Grant on June 4. He said that Grant had never accused Smith of being in a cabal, that Smith's being relieved "came from the impossibility of getting along with General Butler; of the two, you being the junior."(8) The phrase, "you being the junior" implies that Grant had a choice as to who remained and he made the choice based on rank. The statement "the impossibility of (you) getting along with General Butler" implied that Smith was at fault and had to go. It was clear rank played a role in the decision only because it was easier to get rid of Smith than Butler.

General Wilson tells the story that "Grant assured me about this time that it was with great regret that he had taken this action; that he had tried in vain to utilize Smith's great talents; that he [Smith] had been too free in his criticisms, and that Smith himself had made it necessary that either he should be relieved or that Meade, Burnside and Butler should be deprived of command and sent out of the army." (9)

General Franklin, Smith's great friend, offered his explanation for Smith's removal. He wrote to Smith, "The real cause of trouble was Butler's influence over him [Grant]. He is afraid of Butler and always will be, and I see no chance for him." (10) Long after the war, January 23, 1893, General Wistar, a brigade commander in the Eighteenth Corps wrote to General Smith "My Dear General—You have much obliged me by the opportunity to read the proof sheets of your book, ... Your explanation of the manner by which Butler forced a revocation (before it ever saw the light) of the President's order removing him and substituting you as Commander of the Army agrees substantially with what was told me very soon after the event by Hon. John Tucker, Assistant Secretary of War." (11)

When General Godfrey Weitzel (West Point 1855), Commander of the Second Division of the Eighteenth Corps, heard about Smith's misfortune he immediately confronted General Butler. He asked Butler, "Did you have anything at all to do with having General Smith removed? He said promptly, 'No'. Your orders came from an entirely different quarter, or General Butler must have deceived me, which I do not believe." (12)

General Smith's letter to Senator Foot, dated July 20, 1864, was found and published, without Smith's permission after the senator's death. (13) General Butler, in his two volume biography, went to great lengths to refute Smith's allegations in that letter. Butler wrote, "I never saw General Grant drink a glass of spirituous liquor in my life;" (14) In the meeting with Grant about Order 225, Butler said," . . . if I might be permitted to advise, Smith should not be put in charge of the Eighteenth Corps . . ." (15) "The record will show that at thirty minutes past one o'clock p.m. on that Sunday [July 10th.] after Smith had gone, Grant suspended the operation of the order of July 7, and directed that the Eighteenth Army Corps should remain under my command, and that another army corps, the Nineteenth, should be added to my department." (16) "I had not suggested that he be relieved from the army for his misconduct, even after the insulting and garbled correspondence which he sent to Grant in an unmilitary manner." (17)

General Stannard expressed the feelings of the officers and men under Butler. In a letter to Senator Foot, he wrote "Gen. Smith was assigned to the command of the troops and Genl. B to Fortress Monroe by the President, but Genl. B through Lieut. Genl. Grant had the order stayed which was unaccountable to most not supposing for a moment that Genl. Grant would place himself in the power of such a man. We are destined to disappointment. Genl. B. was in company with our Lieut. Genl. at a certain Corps Headquarters where he took to(o) much liquor and from fear of exposure has acceded to his demands and as I understand has promised him a still larger command, which I pray may never take place. We have not sufficient men to march to slaughter." (18)

General Wilson summed it all up, "The undisputable fact is that the countermanding order was issued after a personal interview between Grant and Butler, the details of which are partly known, and that no further explanation consistent with the continuance of friendly relations between Grant and Smith has ever been given." (19)

CHAPTER 31

The End of the War and the Postbellum Period

After he was relieved, General Smith went to New York to await orders. On December 10, 1864, President Lincoln issued an executive order appointing him and the Honorable Henry Stansbery "Special Commissioners to investigate and report, for the information of the President, upon the civil and military administration of the military division bordering upon and west of the Mississippi under such instructions as shall be issued by authority of the President and the War Department." (1)

The Commissioners were based in New Orleans where they investigated the administration of the division which Butler and his successors had headed. They were given broad powers and made several confidential reports which were not made public. (2) One writer states that General Butler "was charged, apparently with justice, with corruption and venality, in conniving at, and sharing, the profits of illicit trade with the Confederates carried on by his brother at New Orleans and by his brother-in-law in the Department of Virginia and North Carolina while General Butler was in command". (3) During this period, on March 13, 1865, General Smith was rewarded and given a brevet promotion to major general. (4)

General Grant became President of the United States in 1878 and served two terms. General Butler served in the Congress as a representative from Massachusetts from 1877-1879. It was in this time period that Butler contacted Smith and proved again that he was 'a damned scoundrel." General Smith wrote," . . . . General Butler prepared a savage attack upon General Grant, of which he showed me the proof-sheets, and in which he invited me to join. I declined. Short passages from this attack were published in the newspapers. Subsequently, a synopsis of the pamphlet was prepared to be sent by the Associated Press throughout the country. Thereupon General Grant sent for General Butler, peace was made, the pamphlet was not published, and General Butler became one of General Grant's most earnest supporters in Congress, and is said to have controlled the distribution of federal offices in Massachusetts; and General Grant thereafter spoke mildly of General Butler's faults." (5) (6)

In May, 1873, General Smith was appointed to the position of police commissioner in New York City. Then, on December 31, 1873, he was appointed to the position of president of the police board and served in that capacity for almost eight years. He spent his efforts in trying to improve the police service, but in the process he alienated the politicians, including the mayor, and was too honest and independent to continue. He resigned on March 11, 1881. (7)

In 1880 General Winfield Scott Hancock, Smith's good friend, was the Democratic nominee for president. Smith and Franklin were very active in supporting him. They attended the Democratic Convention, and did everything they could to aid him in the campaign. In the end, Hancock was not successful, losing to General James Garfield in a fairly close race. (8)

Baldy Smith became a prolific author in the 1880's and 1890's. Most of his writings were about his experiences in the Civil War in both the East and the West. But he also wrote to defend himself from attacks by Butler and Horace Porter.

In 1897, General Horace Porter, who had been a member of U.S. Grant's staff, published an attack on General Smith in a series called "Campaigning with Grant". The attack was for his actions before Petersburg on June 15, 1864". Smith read the article and started to prepare a rebuttal.

While working on his response, Smith received a letter from Thomas S. Baird, who had been the sergeant in charge of the Spring Hill Signal Station during the battle of June 15, 1864. That station was responsible for relaying messages from General Butler to General Smith. Sergeant Baird remembered that "while the fight was going on he had *received from the headquarters station a message from General Butler to me to the effect that I was to cease fighting or firing—entrench at once and hold my position.*" Baird considered the message so important that he mounted his horse and personally delivered it to General Smith. The general, apparently so ill, had no recollection of the event. He did stop the fighting and entrenched shortly after the time the message was received.

Sergeant Baird did not give up. He located a former signalman Maurice S. Lamprey, who had been the sergeant in charge at the Cobb's Hill (Butler's Headquarters) Signal Station on June 15, 1864. Lamprey recorded in his diary, "Send (Sent) message to General Smith to entrench at once and hold his position. Guess Gen. B. is getting rattled over the dust the rebs are kicking up." General Smith went to great lengths to research Baird's and Lamprey's documentations and was able to validate them.

No copy of Butler's message survived in the official records. Smith contended that Butler or his signal officer, Lt. David G. Craft, destroyed their copy so that the decision to stop fighting and entrench would seemingly be Smith's and not Butler's. History and historians have accepted that premise and Smith was blamed for the failure to take Petersburg on June 15, 1864. As Dr. Herbert Schiller, who edited Smith's autobiography, points out, "If Smith's account is correct, and the information came to him through no action of his own,—then the story of his 'failure' before Petersburg on June 15, 1864 clearly must be reevaluated" (9)

After the presidential campaign of 1880 General Smith was forced to return to work for he had made some bad investments. Major General Horatio G. Wright was Chief Engineer of the Army at that time and was responsible for carrying out a plan of Internal Improvements approved and funded by the Congress. In 1881 Wright appointed his friend and former superior, General Smith, government agent in charge of engineering work in the peninsula between the Delaware River and the Chesapeake Bay. His headquarters were in Wilmington, Delaware. He served in that capacity until March 1, 1889. (10)

In 1888 the military committee of the House of Representatives, on its own initiative, took action to place General Smith on the retired list thus giving him a pension. The committee submitted a highly favorable report and recommended that he be placed on the list as a major general. The full house approved the recommendation and sent it to the Senate. The Senate committee approved the bill but cut Smith's rank on the list to major, his rank in the Regular Army. The legislation was enacted giving Smith a pension based on his rank as major. Feeling rebuffed by the Senate, Smith's initial reaction was to decline the annuity but his friends persuaded him to accept it. (11)

The crowning insult for General Smith came when General Rosecrans, and not Smith, was given credit for saving the Army of the Cumberland at Chattanooga in 1863. The Chickamauga and Chattanooga National Park Commission had been established and was headed by Major General H. V. Boynton, formerly an officer in the Army of the Cumberland under Rosecrans. The Commission published an atlas with the following legend:

> **"At daylight of October 27 the river line of the communication with Bridgeport was opened by the execution of a plan for recovering Lookout Valley devised by General Rosecrans, approved by General Thomas, and ordered executed by General Grant under the immediate command of Brig. Gen. W.F. Smith."**

General Smith was incensed when he learned about the legend and wrote to the Park Commission in 1895 in protest. The appeal would continue for six years. Smith was not satisfied with General Boynton's replies of 1895 and 1896 and appealed to Secretary of War Alger. Extensive correspondence followed and finally, at Smith's request, Secretary Alger appointed, under a War Department Order dated August 23, 1900, a board of three officers to investigate the issue and report on it. (12)

The board was chaired by Major General John R. Brooke. It received extensive documentation from Smith and his supporters and Boynton and his supporters. In addition, the board poured over maps of the Brown's Ferry area for the period and visited the site. Toward the end of the review General Smith became ill and was represented by the Honorable Anthony Higgins.

Finally the board issued its findings and reported that '**it failed to find any evidence that Gen. W.F. Smith was the originator of the plan for the relief of Chattanooga by military operations conducted in Lookout Valley, October 1863.**" Secretary of War Elihu Root approved the report on February 16, 1901.

General James Wilson, Smith's friend and biographer, wrote in 1904, ".....Grant, Thomas, and all other officers [including himself] who were present and in a position to know what was actually done gave Smith the praise, not only for conceiving it, but carrying the plan into successful effect, there is but little room left for further controversy." (13)

General Winfield Scott Hancock died on February 12, 1886. General Smith joined numerous other Civil War generals as honorary pallbearers at his military funeral. (14) On May 21, 1901, another good friend, General Fitz John Porter, passed away. Again, General Smith was called upon to be an honorary pallbearer in the military funeral. (15)

General William Farrar Smith followed his comrades when he died in his home in Philadelphia on February 28, 1903. He was buried in Arlington Cemetery with full military honors. (16)

CHAPTER 32

Obituary of Major General William F. Smith

(Courtesy of the Vermont Historical Society)

William Farrar Smith, also known as Baldy Smith, was born in St. Albans, Vermont, February 17, 1824, the son of Ashbel and Sarah Butler Smith. He was educated locally until appointed to the Military Academy at West Point in 1841. He graduated in 1845 as was commissioned as brevet second lieutenant in the Corps of Topographical Engineers. He served in the Corps making surveys of the Great Lakes, Texas, Arizona, Mexico and Florida. While in Florida he became severely ill with malaria, and although he recovered, it affected his health for the rest of his life. In 1856 he became involved in the light-house service, headquartered in Detroit, and eventually became Engineer Secretary of the Light-House Board. During his early career, Smith also taught mathematics at West Point, which allowed him to learn more about military history and warfare than his otherwise scientific career provided him.

Because of his knowledge of the south, acquired through surveying and through his work protecting southern light houses, in 1861, at the outbreak of the Civil War, Smith was sent to Fortress Monroe as an engineer officer to do reconnaissance work around Yorktown and Big Bethel, but had to leave that position because of his health. He was then commissioned as Colonel of the Third Regiment of Vermont Volunteer Infantry, and was instrumental in arranging to have the Vermont regiments trained together as one brigade, rather than joined with regiments from other states. He was named Brigadier-General in August of 1861 and almost immediately was given charge of the Second

Division of the IV Corps, Army of the Potomac. In June 1862 he was brevetted lieutenant colonel in the regular army and a month later became major-general and commanded the Second Division of the VI Corps, at Antietam, and was brevetted colonel. After Fredericksburg he and William Buel Franklin wrote to Lincoln complaining of the leadership in the military and objecting to the plan of war and offering an alternative. Because of that he was transferred and was not given the commission of major-general but reverted to brigadier general. In October of 1863, Smith went to Chattanooga as chief engineer and by March 1864 was re-appointed major general. He was then assigned to the XVIII Corps under Benjamin Franklin Butler but because of tension between Butler and Smith, he was relieved of his command. In March of 1865 Smith was brevetted brigadier general [in the regular army] and major general for his distinguished services at Chattanooga and in the Virginia Campaign of 1864.

He resigned from the volunteers in 1865 and from the regular army in 1867. Smith applied his engineering expertise in the private sector as president of the International Ocean Telegraph company until 1873. After spending a couple of years in Europe he went to New York City and became president of the Board of Police Commissioners until his resignation in 1881. He spent the rest of his life working on various engineering projects for the government (in 1889 he was restored to the military as major), and writing about his service in the Civil War.

His publications include: Military Operations Around Chattanooga (1886); articles for Battles and leaders of the Civil war (four volumes 1887-1888)The Relief of the Army of the Cumberland, and the Opening of the Short Line of Communication between Chattanooga, Tennessee, and Bridgeport, Alabama, in October, 1863, Wilmington, Delaware; C.F. Thomas and Co. 1891 (973.741 Cs) From Chattanooga to Petersburg Under Generals Grant and Butler a Contribution to the History of the War, and a Personal Vindication, Boston: Houghton Mifflin and Co.1893 (973,741 J23s) and the Re-opening of the Tennessee River Near Chattanooga, October 1863 as Related by Major General George H. Thomas and the Official Record compiled an annotated by Bv't Major General W.F. Smith, Wilmington, Delaware: Press of Mercantile Printing Co. 1895.

William Farrar Smith married Sarah Ward Lyon of New York City, in April 1861. They had five children, only two of whom survived their parents; Clara and Stuart Farrar. Smith died in Philadelphia in 1903.

Vermont in the Civil War—Vermont born Generals

Gen. Smith was always a favorite with his soldiers, and although he never joined the Grand Army of the Republic, he retained their affection as veterans. He wrote many military papers, criticisms of a technical nature. He was a member of the Sons of the American Revolution.

APPENDIX No. 1

Medical History—Major General William F. Smith

William Farrar Smith Born February 17, 1824, in St. Albans, Vermont. He graduated from the USMA in 1845. Served in the Florida wars. In 1855 he contracted malaria, which precipitated attacks of chills and fever the rest of his life. During the same year, he also had insolation (sunstroke). He was made colonel of the 3rd. Vermont to rank from July 1861and was promoted to brigadier general in

August. He had typhoid fever in October 1861 and did not resume command until December. On April 16, 186, at Lee's Mill, his horse was going full speed and stepped into a hole. Smith was thrown to the ground and was dazed for the rest of the day. He went on sick leave in July. On January 23, 1863, there was an order stating that Smith could give no further service to the army; Smith was temporarily relieved from duty but no reason was given. He had irritability of the urinary bladder in April, which his surgeon attributed to sitting in the saddle. During May his surgeon stated that he had a tendency to congestion of the brain when subjected to hot summer weather. In June he reported for duty at Hagerstown, Maryland. He had a boil on his arm in July. Smith was relieved at his own request in August and returned in October. In June 1864 he had fever and weakness, which he attributed to sleeping on low, wet ground and drinking the swamp water at Cold Harbor. By the he fifteenth he had such bad dysentery that he could hardly stay on his horse. On July 1 he was in such poor health that he had to ask for a short leave of absence. The trouble was with his head, which, during the heat of the day caused him to feel quite helpless, and he was unable to go out even to visit his lines. Similar problems had driven him from the southern climate three times before. Initially, U S. Grant had refused the leave, but later, after a repeat request, the leave was granted. Smith left on July 9 and returned in ten days. During December 1865 he had a painful knee. He resigned his volunteer commission in1865 and his regular commission in1867. After the war he was president of a cable company, civilian engineer for the government, and a prolific author. From 1871 through 1879 he was treated in Europe and New York for recurring attacks of chills and fever considered to be due to chronic malaria. He had chronic enlargement of the spleen accompanied with congestion of the liver. Died February 28, 1903, in Philadelphia and was buried in Arlington National Cemetery.

Death Certificate: Cause of death, nephritis.
(Welsh, Jack D. Medical Histories of Union Generals, Kent, Ohio Kent State University Press
1996)

Appendix No. 2

General Smith re: General Burnside and Fredericksburg
December, 1862

(On the 17ᵗʰ. of February, 1863, General William F. Smith completed a sworn statement about General Burnside's reactions and comments about the Battle of Fredericksburg. This statement is of utmost significance in understanding Burnside's leadership in that battle. Because it is so important, this appendix is devoted to presenting Smith's statement in its entirety The original of the statement is in the Vermont Historical Collections and is reproduced here with the Society's permission.)

"A Statement made by General William F. Smith this fourteenth day of February, 1863."

In the month of December last I was in command of the Sixth Corps of the Army of the Potomac under the command of Major General Burnside. General Franklin was in command of the Left Grand Division which comprised the First Corps under the command of Major General John Reynolds and the Sixth Corps under my command.

I was made acquainted with the fact of an intended crossing of the Rappahannock some six or seven days before the crossing took place which was on December 12ᵗʰ

After we were made acquainted with the place where the Left Grand Division was to cross we made an examination of the maps and from them and such other sources of information as were within our power, were all of opinion that the place indicated for our crossing was the best from which to make the attack in force.

We crossed on the 11th and 12[th]of December and by one o'clock on the 12th Genl. Franklin's Division was posted in line of battle and the fact reported to Genl. Burnside. The Corps under my command crossed first and was posted before12 o'clock, and after the fog lifted, between one and two o'clock. I examined the country immediately in front of us as well, under the circumstances as was in my power, which examination strengthened the opinion already entertained by Genl. Franklin and myself that an attack in force would and should be made from our left front. This was the subject of conversation between Genl. Franklin and myself in the course of the afternoon and I distinctly remember, and his opinion was decidedly expressed.

Genl. Burnside came to Genl. Franklin's Headquarters before sunset, when our views were expressed to Genl. Burnside in a full conversation on the subject, to which I supposed he assented. Our suggestion was that the attack should be in force, made early in the morning before the fog lifted and thus screen our troops to some extent from the enemy's artillery.

I was present at the entire interview from the time Genl. Burnside reached Genl. Franklin's Headquarters, till he left, which lasted a full hour, and during that time no suggestion was made by Genl. Franklin at variance with the above views, and up to the time Genl. Burnside left, he said nothing to induce me to suppose that he dissented from them. Genl. Franklin more than once requested Genl. Burnside to send him his orders at once, and he replied that they should be sent in two or three hours.

After he left, Genl. Franklin, Genl. Reynolds & myself occupied the same tent, none of undressed and waited through the night anxiously for orders. Before morning Genl. Franklin sent an aide, to Headquarters for orders and made all the arrangements in his power for the execution of the orders, based upon the supposition that the orders would be for an attack in force.

The order reached Genl. Franklin while I was present after seven o'clock in the morning, and was in these words, 'Make your attack with not less than one division, well supported . . . .' General Franklin showed the order immediately to Genl. Reynolds and myself, and the conclusion of all of us was that Genl. Burnside determined not to adopt the plan of making the attack in force from the left.

Long before the order came however, the delay in its arrival was the subject of conversation between us, and that in consequence of it the chances of a successful attack had greatly diminished. No one differed in what was intended by the order, and that was to send a division to be well supported, and immediately upon its receipt Genl. Franklin prepared to carry out the order. He ordered Genl. Reynolds with his corps of three divisions to carryout the order.

His corps was posted with Genl. Meade on the left, Genl. Gibbon on the right, and Genl. Doubleday in reserve. Genl. Meade was ordered by Genl. Reynolds to move his division towards the point indicated in the order. Genl. Gibbon was ordered to support him closely on the right, and Genl. Doubleday was left in reserve to be used as circumstances might require.

Shortly after Meade advanced, the enemy's cavalry appeared on the left accompanied by artillery, and Genl. Reynolds was obliged to order Genl. Doubleday to drive the enemy's cavalry away. I heard a staff officer of Genl. Reynolds inform Genl. Franklin that owing to the cavalry threatening his left, he had been obliged to order Doubleday out there.

Genl. Franklin immediately sent to Genl. Stoneman with one of his divisions & to report himself in person to Genl. Franklin. Before the division reached the field Genl. Franklin ordered its commanding general to report to Genl. Reynolds. Before the first division crossed a similar order was sent by Genl. Franklin to a second division to cross, and before that division crossed, I was ordered to send a division which I had held in reserve to report to Genl. Reynolds. These orders were all executed with promptness and dispatch. From the time the order was received till Genl. Meade was under motion not over fifteen minutes elapsed. The first time I rode down my line Gibbon had moved his division in support of Meade to a point about five hundred yards in front of my line.

I first saw Genl. Burnside after the engagement on Sunday at his Headquarters where the battle was a subject of discussion. He made no intimation of dissatisfaction with Genl. Franklin or any of the operations on the left nor did he intimate that his orders to Genl. Franklin had been either disobeyed or misconstrued.

At that time he said he had intended to take the 9th. Corps and lead in person, but that the statement of generals in command of troops on the right with respect to their demoralization compelled him to abandon the idea. He impressed the idea upon my mind of his conviction of the officers being demoralized. I told him I would promise to take the Sixth Corps against the enemy, and that there was no demoralization among the officers of that corps that would stop them. He also stated that Genl. Franklin was the only officer who supported him in his idea of an attack with the 9th, Corps.

I did not see Genl. Burnside again before we recrossed. Shortly after that I saw Genl. Burnside at his Head Quarters when the subject of the battle of Fredericksburgh was spoken of, and Genl. Burnside told me, while speaking of the battle that he had it in his mind to relieve Gen. Sumner, place Genl. Hooker in arrest, and place Genl. Franklin in command of the army.

A few days after this I had an interview with Genl. Burnside in the presence of Genl. Reynolds in which for the first time he made a word of complaint of the operations on the left. He said the men did not fight well enough. I replied I thought the list of the killed and wounded proved to the contrary of that. He replied he did not mean that he meant that not enough muskets had been fired, and added, I made a mistake in my order to Genl. Franklin. I should have ordered him to have carried the hill at Capt. Hamilton's at all hazards.

The next time that the operations on the left were the subject of conversation he stated that the mistake was that Franklin did not get the order early enough, that he had started it at four o'clock but that Genl. Hardie to whom the order was committed had stopped an hour and a half in the camp to get his breakfast.(*Note: The order was dated 5;55 A.M on December 13, 1862 (ORXXI p.71)*

I then said the grave mistake was certainly in not sending the order early enough to which he responded Yes it should have been there by 12 o'clock. I replied, that was not early enough, that the order might have been sent there to arrive before the troops were fixed for the night, that would have given Genl. Franklin time to have relieved my command by Stoneman's troops and before daylight to have formed a column of attack consisting of Reynold's Corps and my own of over 40,000 men & that such an attack would probably have succeeded' I thought so at that time, that is if Genl. Franklin had received an order such as Genl. Burnside said he should have sent,—to carry the hill at all hazards,—with such a disposition of his troops it could have been done.

But since Genl. Hooker has been in command I have seen a map sent to me by Genl. Butterfield, made by the topographical officer of the Rebel Genl. Jackson;s command giving the position of Jackson's troops opposite our line.—Since seeing that, I am fully of opinion that the only possible chance of our success on that day lay in making such an attack as I have indicated & with at least the force indicated.

Sworn to and subscribed before me this 17th day of February, 1863
Wm. J. Riblet   Wm. F. Smith
Com.(?) of Deeds   Maj. Genl. Vols.
(undecipherable line)

On the back of the statement are these words:

Affidavit especially drawn up for publication with Franklin's papers

Fredericksburg, 1862 Dec. 13th

APPENDIX No. 3

To the PRESIDENT:

The undersigned, holding important commands in the Army of the Potomac, impressed with the belief that a plan of operations of this army may be devised which will be crowned with success, and that the plan of campaign which has already been commenced cannot possibly be successful present, with diffidence, the following view for considerations. Whether the plan proposed be adopted or not, they consider it their duty to present these views, thinking that, perhaps, they may be suggestive to some other military mind in discussing plans for the future operations of our armies in the East.

1. We believe that the plan of campaign already commenced will not be successful for following reasons: First. The distance from this point to Richmond is 61 miles. It will be necessary to keep our communications with Aquia Creek Landing from all points of this route. To effect this, the presence of large bodies of troops on the road will be necessary at many points. The result of making these detachments would be that the enemy will attack them, interrupt the communications, and the army will be obliged to return to drive them away. If the railroad be rebuilt as the army marches, it will be destroyed at important points by the enemy. Second. If we do not depend on the railroad, but by wagon transport, the trains will be so enormous that a great deal of strength of the army will be required to guard the, and the troops will be so separated by trains, and the roads so

blocked by them, that the advance and rear of the army could not be within supporting distance of each other.

2. It is in the power of the enemy at many points on this route to post himself strongly and defy us. The whole strength of our army may not be sufficient to drive him away, and even were he driven away, at great sacrifice of blood on our part, the result would not be decisive. The losses to him in his strong positions would be comparatively slight, while ours would be enormous.

3. In our opinion, any plan of campaign, to be successful, should possess the following requisites, viz: First. All of the troops available in the East should be massed. Second. They should approach as near to Richmond as possible without an engagement. Third. The line of communication should be absolutely free from danger of interruption.

A campaign on the James River enables us to fulfill all of these conditions more absolutely than any other, for—

1. On the James River our troops from both north and south can be concentrated more rapidly than they can be at any other point.

2. They can be brought to points within 20 miles of Richmond without risk of engagement.

3. The communication by the James River can be keep up by the assistance of the Navy without the slightest danger of interruption.

Some of the details of this plan are the following:

We premise that by concentrating our troops in the East we will be able to raise 250,000. Let them be landed on both sides of the river, as near Richmond as possible, 150,000 on the north bank, and 100,000 or more on the south bank, all of them to carry three days' provisions on their persons, and 100 rounds of ammunition, without any other baggage than blankets and shelter tents and a pair of socks and a pair of drawers. Let it be understood that every third day a corps or grand division is provisioned from the river. If this arrangement be practicable (and we think it is), we get rid of all baggage, provisions, and infantry ammunition wagons and the only vehicles will be the artillery and its ammunition wagons and the ambulances. The mobility of the army caused by carrying out these views, will be more like an immense partisan corps than a modern army. The two armies marching up the banks may meet the enemy on or near the river. By means of pontoon, kept afloat, and towed so as to be reached at any point, one army can in few hours cross to assist the other. It is hardly supposable that the enemy can have a force enough to withstand the shock of two such bodies. If the enemy decline to flight on the river, the army on the south bank, or a portion of it, will take possession of the railroads running south from Richmond, while the remainder will proceed to the investment or attack upon Richmond, according to circumstances. Whether the investment of Richmond leads to the destruction or capture of the enemy's army or not, it certainly will lead to the capture of the rebel capital, and the war will be on better footing than it is now or has any present prospect of being. The troops available for the movement are the Army of the Potomac, the troops in Florida, South Carolina, and North Carolina, with the exception of those necessary to hold the places occupied, the regiments now in the process of organization, and those who are on extra duty and furlough, deserters and straggles. The number of these last is enormous, and the most stringent measures must be taken to collect them. No excuse should be received for absence. Some of the troops in Western Virginia might also be detached. The transports should consist of ordinary steamers and large ferry-boats and barges. The ferry-boats may become the greatest use in transporting troops across the James River. With the details of the movement we do not trouble you. Should the general idea be adopted, these can be thoroughly digested and worked out by the generals and their staffs to whom the execution of the plan is committed.

Very respectfully, your obedient servants,
W. B. FRANKLIN
Major-General, Commanding Left Wing.
WM. F. SMITH
Major-General, Commanding Sixth Army Corps.

(O.R., 21, pp. 868-870)

Appendix No. 4

Hon. S. Foot
  Dear Sir
    I take this occasion to communicate with you on the within subject giving you a fair statement in relation to the present condition of our army. So far as my information extends, the Major Genl. Comdg this Department has not the confidence, to say nothing about the respect of a single officer or man (leaving out his immediate hirelings) in the whole Department, meaning the 10th, & 18th.Corps. I have had a good opportunity to learn the feelings that exists in both corps having served in each. The officers, from Generals down, have no delicacy in saying that they do not consider him capable of commanding even so small a force and much more two Corps. And that they do not consider any such Criminal Lawyer qualified to lead such troops as comprise the two Corps. I still hold the opinion (that perhaps you have heard many express) that no Genl. could properly fight his command unless he gave his personal attention to the situation and location in order that he may take advantage of the position to gain the greatest possible advantage with the smallest possible loss. I might here state that Genl. Smith is always there. I say this from actual knowledge. I have never known the Cmdy/ Genl.B. to be at the front, or be in sight of a rebel and I have no recollection of having seen him, with one or two exceptions and that at a distance, since I reported to him on the 11th. Day of May, last. I can only account for this by my having been at the front and in face of the

enemy. Another matter in connection I cannot refrain from mentioning, which is this, When riding about the different camps, in rear of our lines he has mounted men as an advance guard at some distance in front, with carbines at a ready, and while in camp a Detachment of Infantry as Picket at his Headquarters which only creates amusement for officers and ridicule from the men. You will see by this that the army have not even respect, to say nothing about confidence in their Commanding Genl.

I think I relate the feelings of all the officers and men in this command when I say that they have the utmost confidence in Genl. Smith, and nothing could possibly please them more than to be under the command untrammeled by any such officer as our present commander.

Genl. Smith was assigned to the command of the troops and Genl. B. to Fortress Monroe by the President, but Genl. B. through Lieut. Genl. Grant had the order stayed. Which, was unaccountable to most not supposing for a moment that Genl. Grant would place himself in the power of such a man We are destined to disappointment. Genl B. was in company with our Lieut. Genl. At a certain Corps Headquarters when he took to(o) much liquor and from fear of exposure has acceded to his demands and as I understand has promised him a still larger command. Which I pray God may never take place. We have not sufficient men to march to the slaughter.

I have been under the immediate command of Genl. Butler in one campaign. I refer to Drury's Bluff, when if the rebels had fought with their usual tenacity we should have lost our whole command and as it was, if it had not been for the strong argument of Genl. Smith, we should have been annihilated.

Now Senator Foot, I consider the present moment the most propitious of any that our Country has been called to endure, and I cannot help but think any man who has influence and position should put his shoulder to the wheel and help us out of this condition by giving us good and tried men to lead our brave and uncomplaining soldiers, and men too in whom they have confidence who are not afraid to face the rebel hordes notwithstanding the balls fall thick and fast about them. And those who will not sit quietly down and see men murdered without deriving corresponding good results. The thing that has been done to an alarming extent in the last three months, the Commanding

Genl. of the Army of the Potomac has murdered men in the last three months in my estimation to damn any generation, and if this is suffered to go on, I much fear for our country and for her people for whom I have been ready the last three years to lay down my life.

I say frankly and faithfully that I consider Genl. Franklin, Wright, and Smith the best genls in the United States, and those who should command our armies. With such men to lead I should not have the least misgiving in relation to the issue, but as it is I must confess that I have. And God Almighty himself can tell where we should end.

Will you see Genl. Franklin or Smith, I think they corporate every word that I have said, aside from themselves.

In conclusion I will state that that I have found this matter heavy on my mind. And I do it in all confidence. When I say that I believe the war will be continued to an indefinite time under our present commander, I say it in all honesty, and wish to include our Lieut. Genl. and especially Genl. Meade, Commanding the Army of the Potomac of whom I used to be proud.

Will you give of your attention to this vital subject and satisfy yourself. If you find that I am correct, for the credit of our whole country and especially our Green Mountain State, give it the benefit of you superior influence and labor.

This is strictly confidential.

I have the honor to be
Respectfully
Your Obt. Servant

Geo. J. Stannard

₳PPENDIX №. 5

College Point L.I. July 20, 1864

Hon. S. Foote:

Dear Senator,—I am extremely anxious that my friends in my native state should not think that the reason of General Grant's relieving me from duty was brought about by any misconduct of mine, and therefore, I write to put you in possession of such facts in the case as I am aware of, and think will throw light upon the subject. About the very last of June, or the first of July, Generals Grant and Butler came to my headquarters, and shortly after their arrival. General Grant turned to General Butler, and said: "That drink of whiskey I took has done me good". And then, directly afterwards, asked me for a drink. My servant opened a bottle for him, and he drank of it, when the bottle was corked and put away.

I was aware at this time that General Grant had within six months pledged himself to drink nothing intoxicating, but did not feel it would better matters to decline to give it upon his request in General Butler's presence.

After the lapse of an hour or less, the general asked for another drink, which he took. Shortly after, his voice showed plainly that the liquor had affected him, and after a little time he left. I went to see him upon his horse, and as soon as I returned to my tent I said to a staff officer of mine who had witnessed his departure, "General Grant has gone away drunk. General Butler has seen it, and will never fail to use the weapon that has been put into his hands". Two or three days after that I applied for a leave of absence for the benefit of my health, and General Grant sent word to me not to go, if it were possible to stay, and I replied in a private note, warranted by our former relations, a copy of which I will send you in a few days. The next day, the Assistant Secretary of War, Mr. Dana, came to tell me that he had been sent by General Grant that it becomes necessary to repeat in view of subsequent events, to wit: That he, General G. had written a letter the day before, to ask that General Butler might be relieved from that department, July2, and that I placed in command of it, giving as a reason that he could not trust General Butler with the command of troops in the movements about to be made, and saying also, that, next to General Sherman he had more confidence in my ability than that of any general in the field. The order dated July 7, sent General B. to Fortress Monroe, and placed me in command of the troops then under him; and General Grant said he would make the changes necessary to give me the troops in the field belonging to that department. I had only asked that I should not be commanded in battle by a man that could not give an order on the field, a I had recommended General Franklin or General Wright for the command of the department. I was at the headquarters of General Grant on Sunday, July 10, and there saw General B. but had no conversation with him. After General B. had left I had a confidential conversation with General Gant about changes he was going to make. In this conversation it is proper to state that our personal relations were of the most friendly character. He had listened to and acted upon suggestions made by me on more than one important occasion, I then thought, and still think (whatever General Butler's letter writers may say to the contrary), that he knew that any suggestions I might make for his consideration would be dictated by an intense desire to put down this rebellion, and not from any considerations personal to myself, and that no personal friendships had stood in the way of what I considered my duty with regard to military management, a course not likely to be pursued by a man ambitious of advancement. In this confidential conversation with General Grant, I tried to show him the blunders of the late campaign of the Army of the Potomac and the terrible waste of life that had resulted from what I had considered a want of generalship in its present commander. Among other instances, I referred to the fearful slaughter at Cold Harbor, on the 3d. of June. General Grant went in to the discussion defending General Meade stoutly, but finally acknowledged, to use his own words, "that there had been a butchery at Cold Harbor, but that he had said nothing about it because it could do no good." Not a word was said as to my right to criticize General Meade then, and I left without a suspicion that General Grant had taken it in any other way than it was meant, and I do not think he did misunderstand me.

On my return from a short leave of absence on the 19th of July, General Grant sent for me to report to him, and then told me that he "could not relieve General Butler" and that I had so severely criticized General Meade, he had determined to relieve me from the command of the 18th. Corps and order me to New York City to await orders. The next morning the general gave some other reasons, such as an article in the "Tribune" reflecting on General Hancock, which I had nothing in the world to do with, and two letters, which I had written before the campaign began, to two of General Grant's most devoted friends, urging upon them tp try and prevent him from making the campaign he had just made. These letters sent to General Grant's nearest friends and intended for his eye, necessarily sprang from an earnest desire to serve the man upon whom the country had been depending, and these warnings ought to have been my highest justification in his opinion, and indeed would have been, but that it had become necessary to make out a case against me. All these matters, moreover, were known to the general before he asked that I might be put in command of the Department of Virginia and North Carolina, and therefore they formed no cause for relieving me from the command I held.

I also submit to you that if it had been proven to him that I was unfitted for the command I held, that that in nowise changed the case with reference to General Butler and his incompetency, and did not furnish a reason why he should not go where the President had ordered him at the request of General Grant; and that as General Grant did, immediately after an interview with General Butler, suspend the order and announce his intention of relieving me from duty there other reasons must be sought, different from any assigned, for his sudden change of views and action. Since I have been in New York, I have heard from two different sources (one being from General Grant's headquarters and one a staff officer of a general on intimate official relations with General Butler) that General Butler went to General Grant and threatened to expose his intoxication, if the order was not revoked.

I also learned that General Butler had threatened to make public something that would prevent the President's re-election. General Grant told me (when I asked him about General Butler's threat of crushing me) that he had heard that General Butler had made some threat with reference to the Chicago convention, which he (Butler) he said, he has in his "breeches pocket," but General Grant was not clear in expressing what the threat was. I refer to this simply because I feel convinced that the change was not made for an of the reasons that have been assigned; and whether General Butler has threatened General Grant with his opposition to Mr. Lincoln at the coming election, or has appealed to any political aspirations which General Grant may entertain, I do not know; but one thing is certain, I was not guilty of any acts of insubordination between my appointment and my suspension, for I was absent all those days on leave of absence from General Grant. I only hope that this long story will not tire you and that it will convince you that I have done nothing to deserve a loss of confidence which was reposed in me.

Yours very truly,
Wm. F. Smith, Major-General

P.S. I have not referred to the state of things at headquarters when I left, and to the fact that General Grant was then in the habit of getting liquor in a surreptitious manner, because it was not relevant to my case; but if you think, at any time the matter may be of importance to the country, I will give it to you. Should you wish to write to me, please address, care of S.E. Lyon, Jauncy Court, 39 Wall Street, New York.

Wm. F. S.

NOTES

Chapter 1 The Northern Frontier—St. Albans, Vermont

1. James Harrison Wilson, Major General U.S.V., Heroes of the Great Conflict: Life and Services of William Farrar Smith, Major General, United States Volunteer in the Civil War. (Wilmington, Delaware, The John Rogers Press, 1904) p. 4
2. L.L. Ducther, A.M., The History of St. Albans, Vermont, St. Albans, Vermont, Stephen E. Royce, 1872) p. 316
3. James Harrison Wilson, Major General U.S.V., Heroes of the Great Conflict: Life and Services of William Farrar Smith, Major General, United States Volunteer in the Civil War, p.4
4. Ibid. p. 5
5. Walter H. Crockett, History of Vermont (New York, The Century History Company, 1921, volume III p. 299
6. Ibid, p, 298-9
7. James Harrison Wilson, Major General U.S.V., Heroes of the Great Conflict: Life and Services of William Farrar Smith, Major General, United States Volunteer in the Civil War, p.1
8. Ibid. p.5
9. L.L. Ducther, A.M., The History of St. Albans, Vermont, St. Albans, Vermont, p. 299
10. Walter H. Crockett, History of Vermont, volume III, p. 281-285
11. James Harrison Wilson, Major General U.S.V., Heroes of the Great Conflict: Life and Services of William Farrar Smith, Major General, United States Volunteer in the Civil War, p. xxxiii

Chapter 2 West Point and the Pre-War Years

1. George W. Cullum, Biographical Register of the Officers and Graduates of the United States Military Academy at West Point, New York, since its establishment in 1802. (Internet)
2. James Harrison Wilson, Major General U.S.V., Heroes of the Great Conflict: Life and Services of William Farrar Smith, Major General, United States Volunteer in the Civil War, p 8
3. Herbert M. Schiller, ed. Autobiography of Major General William F. Smith, Dayton Ohio. Morningside House, 1990, p. xxiii
4. George W. Cullum, Biographical Register of the Officers and Graduates of the United States Military Academy at West Point, New York, since its establishment in 1802. (Internet)
5. William F. Smith Diary, (Vermont Historical Society)
6. James Harrison Wilson, Major General U.S.V., Heroes of the Great Conflict: Life and Services of William Farrar Smith, Major General, United States Volunteer in the Civil War, p. 2
7. Ibid, p 7
8. Ibid, p.1
9. Ibid, p.8

Chapter 3 Politics and Army Leadership

1. Herbert M. Schiller, ed. Autobiography of Major General William F. Smith, p. xxiii
2. Mark A. Snell, From First to Last, The Life of Major General William B. Franklin, New York, Fordham University Press, 2002 p. 6
3. President and Vice Presidents of the United States, John Tyler, Internet
4. George G. Meade, editor, The Life and Letters of George Gordon Meade New York, Charles Scribner and Sons, 1914 vol. 1, p. 11
5. U.S. Grant, Personal Memoirs of U.S. Grant, New York, Charles Webster and Son, 1885 vol. 1, p. 33
6. James Harrison Wilson, Major General U.S.V., Heroes of the Great Conflict: Life and Services of William Farrar Smith, Major General, United States Volunteer in the Civil War, p 9

7. Mark A. Snell, From First to Last, The Life of Major General William B. Franklin, P.55

8. Stephen A. Sears, George B. McClellan, The Young Napoleon, New York, Tichenor and Fields, 1988 p. 69

9. U.S. Grant, Personal Memoirs of U.S. Grant, New York, Charles L. Webster and Son, 1885 vol. 1, p.238-243

10. Major General George B. McClellan, Report of the Organization of the Army of the Potomac and its Campaigns in Virginia and Maryland, House of Representatives 38th. Congress, 1st. Session, Executive Document No. 15, Washington, D.C. Government Printing Office, 1864, p. 3-5(Hereafter listed as "McClellan's Report)

11. Benjamin P. Thomas, Abraham Lincoln, New York, Alfred A. Knopf, 1952 p. 345

12. Stephen W. Sears, The Young Napoleon, New York, Tichenor and Fields, 1988, p.325

13. O.R. XI part 2, p. 130

14. Mark A. Snell, From First to Last, The Life of Major General William B. Franklin, p.264

15. Fletcher Pratt, Stanton, Lincoln's Secretary of War, New York, W.W. Norton and Company, 1953, p. 351

16. Ibid, p. 350

Chapter 4 The Beginning of the Civil War

1. Bruce Catton, The Coming Fury (New York, Doubleday and Company, 1961) p. 190

2. James Harrison Wilson, Major General U.S.V., Heroes of the Great Conflict: Life and Services of William Farrar Smith, Major General, United States Volunteer in the Civil War, p. 7

3. Ibid, p. 10-11

4. George G. Benedict, Vermont in the Civil War, Burlington, Vermont, The Free Press, 1886-1888, vol.1, p. 130-131

5. Ibid. p. 129-131

6. Theodore S. Peck, Revised Roster of Vermont Volunteers Who Served in the Army or the Navy of the United States During the War of the Rebellion Montpelier, Vermont, Wachtman Company 1872, p. 681

7. McClellan's Report, p. 186
8. Herbert M. Schiller, ed. Autobiography of Major General William F. Smith, p. 30
9. George G. Benedict, Vermont in the Civil War, vol. 1, p.93-95
10. Stephen A. Sears, George B. McClellan, The Young Napoleon, p. 121
11. Ibid. p.144-145
12. Ibid
13. Mark A. Snell, From First to Last, The Life of Major General William B. Franklin, p.76
14. Ibid, p.76 note
15. Alexander Kelly McClure, Annals of the Civil War New York, The DeCapo Press, reprint 1994 p. 79
16. Herbert M. Schiller, ed. Autobiography of Major General William F. Smith, p. 31-32

Chapter 5 The Peninsular Campaign—Lee's Mill

1. Herbert M. Schiller, ed. Autobiography of Major General William F. Smith, p.33
2. Ibid
3. Johnson, Robert U. and Clarence C. Buel, editors, Battles and Leaders of the Civil War (New York, The Century Company, 1884-1887) vol. 2, p.170
4. McClellan's Report p. 75
5. Stephen A. Sears, George B. McClellan, The Young Napoleon, P. 175
6. Ibid. p. 174
7. Alexander Kelly McClure, Annals of the Civil War New York, The DeCapo Press, reprint 1994 p. 81
8. Stephen A. Sears, George B. McClellan, The Young Napoleon, p.166
9. Crafts, W.F.W.A. The Southern Rebellion being a History of the United States from the Commencement of President Buchanan's Administration through the War for the Suppression of the Rebellion.(Boston, Samuel Walker and Co.1868)Vol;.1, P.501(Hereafter listed as Crafts)
10. O.R. XI part 1, p. 42-43

11. McClellan's Report p. 77
12. O.R. XI part 1, p. 1
13. McClellan's Report p.87
14. O.R. XI part 1 p. 405
15. Ibid p.406
16. Herbert M. Schiller, ed. Autobiography of Major General William F. Smith, p. 34-35
17. O.R. XI part 1, p. 364-365
18. Herbert M. Schiller, ed. Autobiography of Major General William F. Smith, p. 35
19. Ibid
20. George G. Benedict, Vermont in the Civil War, vol. 1, p.265-266
21. O.R. XI part 1, p. 275

Chapter 6 The Battle of Williamsburg

1. George G. Benedict, Vermont in the Civil War, vol. p.279
2. O.R. XI part 1, p. 464
3. Ibid., p. 275, 465
4. Ibid 465
5. Herbert M. Schiller, ed. Autobiography of Major General William F. Smith, p. 36
6. Ibid., p.36-37
7. George G. Benedict, Vermont in the Civil War, vol. p.271-273
8. O.R. XI part 3. pp. 133-134
9. Ibid, p. 154-155
10. Ibid
11. McClellan's Report, p. 93
12. Herbert M. Schiller, ed. Autobiography of Major General William F. Smith, p. 39

Chapter 7 Lee Takes Command

1. Emory Thomas, Robert E. Lee, New York, W. W. Morton and Company, 1995, p.226
2. Clifford Dowdey and Louis Manaris, New York, The DeCapo Press, 1961 p. 179

3. Alexander Webb, Campaigns of the Civil War, The Peninsula, New York, Charles Scribner Sons, 1881 p. 115
4. Clifford Dowdey and Louis Manaris, New York, The DeCapo Press, 1961 p. 181
5. Stephen A. Sears, George B. McClellan, The Young Napoleon p. 180
6. Ibid
7. Herbert M. Schiller, ed. Autobiography of Major General William F. Smith p. 33
8. Clifford Dowdey and Louis Manaris, New York, The DeCapo Press, 1961 p. 179-180
9. Robert U. Johnson and Clarence C. Buel, Battles and Leaders of the Civil War, vol.2, p. 324
10. Herbert M. Schiller, ed. Autobiography of Major General William F. Smith p 40-.41
11. Ibid. p. 41
12. Ibid
13. Robert U. Johnson and Clarence C. Buel, Battles and Leaders of the Civil War, vol. 2, p. 334-335
14. Alexander Webb, Campaigns of the Civil War, The Peninsula, p. 134
15. Herbert M. Schiller, ed. Autobiography of Major General William F. Smith, p 41
16. George G. Benedict, Vermont in the Civil War, vol. 1, p.285-287
17. O.R. XI part 2, p. 19
18. Ibid. p.222
19. Webb, p.119-120
20. Robert U. Johnson and Clarence C. Buel, Battles and Leaders of the Civil War Battles and Leaders, vol.2, p.341-342
21. Alexander Webb, Campaigns of the Civil War, The Peninsula Webb, The Peninsula Webb, p.120
22. Robert U. Johnson and Clarence C. Buel, Battles and Leaders of the Civil War, vol. 2. p.381
23. McClellan's Report p. 131
24. Clifford Dowdey and Louis Manaris, New York, The DeCapo Press, 1961 p. 218
25. Lt. General James Longstreet, New York, The DeCapo Press, reprint 1992, p. 130
26. O.R. XI part 2, p. 464

Chapter 8 Covering the Retreat to the James

1. Herbert M. Schiller, ed. Autobiography of Major General William F. Smith, p.42
2. Ibid
3. Ibid
4. Clifford Dowdey and Louis Manaris, New York, The DeCapo Press, 1961, p. 205
5. Herbert M. Schiller, ed. Autobiography of Major General William F. Smith p. 42
6. O.R. XI part 2, p.434
7. Johnson U. Johnson and Clarence C. Buel, Battles and Leaders of the Civil War, vol. 2, p.375
8. Alexander Webb, Campaigns of the Civil War, The Peninsula, p. 480
9. O.R. XI part 2, p. 99
10. Ibid.p.430-431
11. George G. Benedict, Vermont in the Civil War, vol. 1 p.303
12. Herbert M. Schiller, ed. Autobiography of Major General William F. Smith, p. 45
13. O.R. XI part 2, p.464
14. Herbert M. Schiller, ed. Autobiography of Major General William F. Smith, p. 45
15. George G. Benedict, Vermont in the Civil War Benedict vol. 1, p. 304-305
16. Johnson U. Johnson and Clarence C. Buel, Battles and Leaders of the Civil War, vol. 2, p. 317
17. O.R. XI part 2 p. 431
18. Johnson U. Johnson and Clarence C. Buel, Battles and Leaders of the Civil War, vol. 2. p. 388
19. Ibid. p. 379, 381
20. O.R. XI part 2, p. 975-984
21. Herbert M. Schiller, ed. Autobiography of Major General William F. Smith, 47-48
22. James Harrison Wilson, Major General U.S.V., Heroes of the Great Conflict: Life and Services of William Farrar Smith, Major General, United States Volunteer in the Civil War, p. 18-19

23. Herbert M. Schiller, ed. Autobiography of Major General William F. Smit, p. 48

24. Ibid. p. 49

25. Ibid.

Chapter 9 Between Campaigns

1. Herbert M. Schiller, ed. Autobiography of Major General William F. Smith, p.48

2. Ibid. p. 50 note

3. George S. Maharay, The Ever-Changing Leaders and Organization of The Army of the Potomac, New York, iUniverse, 2010, p.30

4. Herbert M. Schiller, ed. Autobiography of Major General William F. Smith, p.50 note

5. Ibid

6. Stephen A. Sears, George B. McClellan, The Young Napoleon, p.227-228

7. O.R. XI part 3, p.314

8. Stephen A. Sears, George B. McClellan, The Young Napoleon p.229

9. Ezra J Warner, Generals in Blue, Baton Rouge, La. Louisiana University Press,1964, p 195-197

10. Herbert M. Schiller, ed. Autobiography of Major General William F. Smith, p. 51

11. O.R. XI part 1, p. 169

12. George S. Maharay, The Ever-Changing Leaders and Organization of The Army of the Potomac, p. 41

13. Crafts, vol.2, p. 22

14. Ibid, p.150-152

15. George S. Maharay, The Ever-Changing Leaders and Organization of The Army of the Potomac, p. 2

16. Mark A. Snell, From First to Last, The Life of Major General William B. Franklin p. 155

17. Fletcher Pratt Stanton, Lincoln's Secretary of War p.230

18. William B. Westervelt, Edited by George S. Maharay. Lights and Shadows of Army Life, Shippensburg, Pa., The Burd Street Press, 1998, p. 32

19. Mark A. Snell, From First to Last, The Life of Major General William B. Franklin, p. 157

20. George S. Maharay, The Ever-Changing Leaders and Organization of The Army of the Potomac, p. 48-49

21. Mark A. Snell, From First to Last, The Life of Major General William B. Franklin, p.164

22. O.R, XII part 2, p. 536

23. Colonel Vincent J. Esposito, The West Point Atlas of the Civil War, New York, Frederick A. Praeger. 1962, Narrative for Map No. 62

24. Herbert M. Schiller, ed. Autobiography of Major General William F. Smith, p. 52 note

25. Major General Fitz John Porter, Internet

26. William B. Westervelt, Edited by George S. Maharay. Lights and Shadows of Army Life, p. 56

27. Stephen A. Sears, George B. McClellan, The Young Napoleon p. 259

Chapter 10 The Return of McClellan

1. Doris Kearns Goodwin, Team of Rivals, New York, Simon and Schuster 2005, p.474

2. Fletcher Pratt Stanton, Lincoln's Secretary of War, p.235

3. Stephen A. Sears, Controversies and Commanders, Dispatches From the Army of the Potomac, Boston, Houghton Mifflin, 1999, p. 90

4. Ibid. p 259-260

5. Fletcher Pratt Stanton, Lincoln's Secretary of War, p. 235

6. Herbert M. Schiller, ed. Autobiography of Major General William F. Smith p. 52

7. O.R. XIX part 2, p. 169

8. Ibid.

9. McClellan's Report, p. 186

10. Ibid p. 188-189

11. O.R. XIX part 2, p.281

12. McClellan's Report p.192

13. Ibid

14. O.R. XIX part 2, p. 870

15. Stephen A. Sears, Landscape Turned Red, New Haven, Ct. Tichenor and Field, 1983 p.146
16. O.R. XIX part 1, p.380
17. Charles Bryant Fairchild, history of the 27th. Regiment, New York Volunteers, Binghamton, N.Y, Carl and Matthews, 1888p. 91
18. James Murfin, The Gleam of Bayonets, New York, Thomas Yoseleff, 1968, p. 374
19. O.R. XIX part 1, p.383
20. Mark A. Snell, From First to Last, The Life of Major General William B. Franklin, p. 183
21. Lt. General James Longstreet, New York, The DeCapo Press, reprint 1992, p. 229-230
22. O.R.XIX part 1, p. 584
23. Ibid. part 2, p.294
24. Ibid, part 1, p. 951
25. Ibid, p. 855
26. Robert U. Johnson and Clarence C. Buel, Battles and Leaders of the Civil War, vol. 2. p.595
27. O.R. XIX part 1, p.639
28. Robert U. Johnson and Clarence C. Buel, Battles and Leaders of the Civil War, vol. 2, p.596
29. George S. Maharay, Vermont Hero, Major General George J. Stannard, Shippensburg, Pa. White Mane Books, 2001, p 94-100

Chapter 11 Antietam and the End of McClellan

1. O.R. XIX part 1, p. 402
2. Ibid
3. Herbert M. Schiller, ed. Autobiography of Major General William F. Smith, P.53
4. Ibid
5. O.R. XIX part 1, p. 402
6. Robert U. Johnson and Clarence C. Buel, Battles and Leaders of the Civil War, vol.2, 593
7. Stephen A. Sears, Landscape Turned Red Sears, p. 27
8. Robert U. Johnson and Clarence C. Buel, Battles and Leaders of the Civil War, vol.2, p. 597

9. Herbert M. Schiller, ed. Autobiography of Major General William F. Smith p 54
10. Robert U. Johnson and Clarence C. Buel, Battles and Leaders of the Civil War, vol. 2, p. 642
11. Stephen A. Sears, Landscape Turned Red Sears, p. 360
12. Robert U. Johnson and Clarence C. Buel, Battles and Leaders of the Civil War, vol. 2, p. 647
13. Ezra J. Warner, Generals in Blue, Baton Rouge, La., Louisiana University Press, 1964 p. 97-98
14. Robert U. Johnson and Clarence C. Buel, Battles and Leaders of the Civil War, vol. 2, p.633
15. Herbert M. Schiller, ed. Autobiography of Major General William F. Smith p.56
16. Ibid p. 59
17. Ibid p. 56
18. Stephen w. Sears, The Young Napoleon. 329
19. William B. Westervelt, Edited by George S. Maharay. Lights and Shadows of Army Life, p.69
20. Charles Carleton Coffin, Four Years of Fighting, Boston, Mass., Tichenor and Fields, 1866, p.137
21. Colonel Vincent J. Esposito, The West Point Atlas of the Civil War, Narrative for Map 70
22. Mark A. Snell, From First to Last, The Life of Major General William B. Franklin, p. 151-152
23. Herbert M. Schiller, ed. Autobiography of Major General William F. Smith p. 57-58
24. O.R. XIX, part 2, p.395-396
25. Herbert M. Schiller, ed. Autobiography of Major General William F. Smith p.58
26. Ibid
27. Ibid p.59
28. Ibid p. 39

Chapter 12 Fredericksburg—Burnside's Plans, November 7-December 12, 1862

1. Fletcher Pratt. Lincoln's Secretary of War, p. 157
2. Ibid

3. John F. Masarek, Commander of all Lincoln's armies, Life of Henry W. Halleck, Cambridge, Mass., Belknap Press, 2004, p. 158, 153

4. Report of the Joint Committee on the Conduct of the War, Washington, D.C., Govt. Printing Office, 1863, part 1, p. 650

5. George S. Maharay, The Ever-Changing Leaders and Organization of the Army of the Potomac p. 87-93

6. T. Harry Williams, Lincoln and His Generals, New York, Alfred A. Knopf, 1952 p. 194

7. O.R. XXI p. 99-101

8. T. Harry Williams, Lincoln and His Generals, p.195

9. Crafts, vol. 2, p.322

10. O.R. XXI p. 85

11. Vincent J. Esposito, The West Point Atlas of the Civil War, Narrative for Map 71

12. Lt. General James Longstreet, From Manassas to Appomattox, p. 293, 299

13. O.R. XXI p. 798

14. T. Harry Williams, Lincoln and His Generals Williams p. 198

15. Ibid

16. Herbert M. Schiller, ed. Autobiography of Major General William F. Smith p. 60

17. Francis A Palfrey, Campaigns of the Civil War, The Antietam and Fredericksburg, New York, Charles Scribner and Sons, 1882, p. 146, 149

18. Ibid p141

19. Emory Thomas, Robert E. Lee, New York, p. 269

20. General Andrew A. Humphreys, The Virginia Campaign, 1854-1865, New York, The De Capo Press, 1995, p. 75

21. Herbert M. Schiller, ed. Autobiography of Major General William F. Smith, P. 61

22. Ibid

23. O.R. XXI p.89

Chapter 13 The Battle of Fredericksburg, December 13, 1862

1. O.R. XXI, p. 450

2. Francis W. Palfrey, Campaigns of the Civil War, The Antietam and Fredericksburg, p. 152-153

3. James Allen Hardie, Memoir of James Allen Hardie, Inspector General, United States Army, Washington, D.C. Kessinger Publishing Legacy Reprints, Originally printed 1877, p. 1
4. Ibid, p.8
5. Ibid, p. 32-33
6. Ibid, p. vii
7. O.R. XXI, p. 71
8. Herbert M. Schiller, ed. Autobiography of Major General William F. Smith,.p. 61
9. Appendix 2, p. 2
10. Report of the Joint Committee on the Conduct of the War, p.708
11. Ibid, p. 710
12. Francis W. Palfrey, Campaigns of the Civil War, The Antietam and Fredericksburg, p. 153-154
13. Colonel Vincent J. Esposito, The West Point Atlas of the Civil War, Narrative for Map 72
14. Report of the Joint Committee on the Conduct of the War, p. 715
15. Ibid., p 714
16. O.R. XXI, p. 109
17. Ibid., p. 91
18. Ibid
19. O.R. XXI, p. 127-128
20. Ibid., p. 95
21. Report of the Joint Committee on the Conduct of the War, p. 667-8
22. Ibid., p. 656
23. Ibid., p. 555
24. Appendix 2

Chapter 14 Fredericksburg—Aftermath. December 14, 1862-May 31, 1863

1. O.R. XXI, p. 67
2. Mark A. Snell, From First to last The Life of Major General William B. Franklin, p.228

3. The Report of the Joint Committee on the Conduct of the War, p. 656
4. Ibid, p. 662
5. Ibid., p. 667
6. Ibid., p. 670
7. Ibid., p.662
8. George S. Maharay, The Ever-Changing Leaders and Organization of the Army of the Potomac, p. 15
9. O.R. XXI, p. 868
10. George S. Maharay, The Ever-Changing Leaders and Organization of the Army of the Potomac, p. 2
11. James Harrison Wilson, Major General U.S.V., Heroes of the Great Conflict: Life and Services of William Farrar Smith, Major General, United States Volunteer in the Civil War, p. 22
12. The Report of the Joint Committee on the Conduct of the War, p.716
13. Ibid., p.730-746
14. O.R. XXI, p 900
15. Ibid., p. 941
16. Ibid., p. 944,945
17. Ibid., footnote, p. 941
18. Ibid. p. 991
19. Ibid., p. 994
20. Ibid., p.998, 999
21. Ibid., p. 1004, 1005
22. Ibid., p. 2, 3, 353
23. Herbert M. Schiller, ed. Autobiography of Major General William F. Smith, p. 66.67
24. George Meade, The Life and Letters of George Gordon Meade, vol. 1, p. 353
25. The Report of the Joint Committee on the Conduct of the War, p. 715-726
26. Ibid. p. 735
27. Ibid. p. 743
28. Herbert M. Schiller, ed. Autobiography of Major General William F. Smith, p.. 67
29. George Meade, The Life and Letters of George Gordon Meade, p. 360

30. The Report of the Joint Committee on the Conduct of the War, p. 57
31. Mark A. Snell, From First to last The Life of Major General William B. Franklin, p.264, 265

Chapter 15 The Gettysburg Campaign, June 10-July 15, 1863

1. O.R. XVIII p. 2
2. Herbert M. Schiller, ed. Autobiography of Major General William F. Smith, p. 66
3. Ibid. xiii, xiv
4. Ibid. p.32
5. O.R. XXVII part 3, p. 54
6. Ibid, p. 55
7. Herbert M. Schiller, ed. Autobiography of Major General William F. Smith. p. 67
8. O.R. XXVII part 3, p. 330
9. Herbert M. Schiller, ed. Autobiography of Major General William F. Smith. p.67
10. Ibid p. 68
11. O.R. XXVII part 3, p.679
12. Ibid p. 508
13. Ibid p. 518
14. Herbert M. Schiller, ed. Autobiography of Major General William F. Smith. p. 69
15. O.R. XXVII part 3 p. 525
16. Ibid p. 526
17. Ibid p. 527
18. Ibid, p.548
19. Ibid p. 551
20. Ibid, part 1, p.80, part 3, p. 579
21. Ibid p. 579
22. Ibid p. 566
23. Ibid p. 580
24. Ibid p. 585
25. Ibid p. 611
26. Ibid p.622,633,635.654
27. Ibid p. 633

28. Ibid p. 686
29. bid p. 703
30. Ibid p. 704

Chapter 16 Aftermath of the Gettysburg Campaign: Politics and Command, July 15-August 26 1863

1. O.R. XXVII, part 3, p. 698
2. Ibid p. 705
3. Ibid p. 715-716
4. Fletcher Pratt, Stanton, Lincoln's Secretary of War, p. 309, 310
5. Herbert M. Schiller, ed. Autobiography of Major General William F. Smith, p. 70
6. James Harrison Wilson, Major General, U.S.V. Heroes of the Great Conflict, Life ad Services of William Farrar smith, Major General, United States Volunteer in the Civil War, p. 23
7. O.R. XXVII, part 3, p. 719, 720, 722
8. Ibid. p, 725
9. Ibid p. 737
10. Ibid p 737, 738, 746, 747, 750, 757
11. Ibid p.736
12. Ibid p. 747, 748
13. Ibid p. 749
14. Ibid p. 814
15. Ibid p. 757, 758
16. Ibid p. 758
17. Ibid p. 764, 771
18. Ibid p.837, 838
19. O.R. XXIX p. 102
20. Herbert M. Schiller, ed. Autobiography of Major General William F. Smith p. 70

Chapter 17 Chattanooga, September 30-October 19, 1863

1. Herbert M. Schiller, ed. Autobiography of Major General William F. Smith, p.70, 71
2. Colonel Vincent J Esposito, The West Point Atlas of the Civil War, Map 115

3. Ibid. Maps 111-115
4. Herbert M. Schiller, ed. Autobiography of Major General William F. Smith, p.71
5. O.R. XXX part 1, p. 215
6. Ibid. part 4, p.62
7. Ibid p. 254
8. Robert U. Johnson & Clarence C. Buel, Battles and Leaders of the Civil War, vol.3, p. 685
9. Ibid, p. 686-687
10. Herbert M. Schiller, ed. Autobiography of Major General William F. Smith, p.72
11. Ibid
12. Benjamin Thomas, Abraham Lincoln, p. 395
13. Fletcher Pratt, Stanton, Lincoln's Secretary of War, p. 323
14. O.R. XXIX part 1, p. 150
15. Herbert M. Schiller, ed. Autobiography of Major General William F. Smith, p. 73-74
16. Ibid p.74
17. O.R. XXX part 1, p.5

Chapter 18 "The Cracker Line", October 20-28, 1863

1. Robert U. Johnson & Clarence C. Buel, Battles and Leaders of the Civil War, vol 3, p 681-682
2. Ibid
3. Ibid p. 683
4. Herbert M. Schiller, ed. Autobiography of Major General William F. Smith. p.72
5. Robert U. Johnson & Clarence C. Buel, Battles and Leaders of the Civil War, vol. 3, p. 684,685
6. Herbert M. Schiller, ed. Autobiography of Major General William F. Smith, p. 74
7. Robert U. Johnson & Clarence C. Buel, Battles and Leaders of the Civil War, vol.3, p. 685
8. Ibid. p. 687
9. Ibid
10. O.R. XXXI part 1. p. 83-85

11. Robert U. Johnson & Clarence C. Buel, Battles and Leaders of the Civil War, vol. 3, p. 688
12. O.R. XXXI part 1, p.97
13. Ibid, p. 58
14. Ibid. p. 72

Chapter 19 The Chattanooga Campaign, October 28-December 4, 1863

1. O.R. XXXI part 1, 68
2. Herbert M. Schiller, ed. Autobiography of Major General William F. Smith, p 77
3. O.R. XXXI part 1, 77
4. Ibid., p. 112-120
5. Herbert M. Schiller, ed. Autobiography of Major General William F. Smith, p. 77
6. Ibid, p. 73
7. Robert U. Johnson and Clarence C. Buel, Battles and Leaders of the Civil War, vol.3, p. 689
8. Herbert M. Schiller, ed. Autobiography of Major General William F. Smith, p. 77
9. O.R. XXXI part 1, p. 74
10. Robert U. Johnson and Clarence C. Buel, Battles and Leaders of the Civil War, vol.3, p.689
11. Ibid. p. 693
12. Ibid. p.752
13. Ibid p. 693, 694
14. O.R. XXXI part 2, p. 57
15. Robert U. Johnson and Clarence C. Buel, Battles and Leaders of the Civil War, vol.3, p. 694
16. Herbert M. Schiller, ed. Autobiography of Major General William F. Smith, p. 78
17. Robert U. Johnson and Clarence C. Buel, Battles and Leaders of the Civil War, vol.3, p. 694
18. Herbert M. Schiller, ed. Autobiography of Major General William F. Smith, p. 78
19. Colonel Vincent J. Esposito, The West Point Atlas of the Civil War, Map 116

20. Herbert M. Schiller, ed. Autobiography of Major General William F. Smith, p. 79
21. Robert U. Johnson and Clarence C. Buel, Battles and Leaders of the Civil War, vol.3, p. 695, 696,
22. O.R. XXXI part 3, p. 123
23. Ibid., part 2, p. 74, 75
24. Ibid., p. 589, 590
25. Ibid., p. 32
26. Ibid., p. 572
27. Robert U. Johnson and Clarence C. Buel, Battles and Leaders of the Civil War, vol.3, p. 716
28. O.R. XXXI part 2, p. 589, 590
29. Ibid., p. 75
30. Ibid., p. 572
31. O.R. XXXI, part. 2, p. 33, 34
32. Robert U. Johnson and Clarence C. Buel, Battles and Leaders of the Civil War, vol.3, p. 717
33. Herbert M. Schiller, ed. Autobiography of Major General William F. Smith, p. 80
34. Ibid, p. 80, 81
35. Robert U. Johnson and Clarence C. Buel, Battles and Leaders of the Civil War, vol 3, 714-718
36. Colonel Vincent J. Esposito, The West Point Atlas of the Civil War, Map 116
37. Herbert M. Schiller, ed. Autobiography of Major General William F. Smith, p. 81
38. Ibid., footnote p. 81
39. O.R. XXXI, part 1, p. 251
40. Robert U. Johnson and Clarence C. Buel, Battles and Leaders of the Civil War, vol 3, p, 693-695
41. Ibid
42. Herbert M. Schiller, ed. Autobiography of Major General William F. Smith, p. 82
43. O.R. XXXI, part 1, p. 265
44. Herbert M. Schiller, ed. Autobiography of Major General William F. Smith, p. 82
45. O.R. XXXI, part 2, p. 524

Chapter 20 Accolades for General Smith, Hooker's Criticism, December 5, 1863-March 26, 1864

1. O.R. XXXI part 3, p. 122
2. Ibid p. 122
3. Ibid p. 201
4. Ibid p. 277
5. Ibid p. 458
6. Ibid p. 571
7. Ibid, part 2 p.80
8. Ibid p. 467,468
9. Herbert M. Schiller, ed. Autobiography of Major General William F. Smith, p.83
10. Fletcher Pratt, Stanton, Lincoln's Secretary of War, p. 350, 351

Chapter 21 Butler—The Damnedest Scoundrel, March 3, 1864-April 29, 1864

1. Herbert M. Schiller, ed. Autobiography of Major General William F. Smith. p. 83
2. U.S. Grant, Personal Memoirs of U.S. Grant, New York, Charles Webster & Son, 1885-1886 Grant's memoirs, vol. 2, p.133
3. James Harrison Wilson, Major General USV, Heroes of the Great conflict, Life and Services of William Farrar Smith, United States Volunteer in the Civil War, p. 32
4. U.S. Grant, Personal Memoirs of U.S. Grant, New York, vol. 2, p.133
5. O.R. XXXII p. 99-101
6. O.R. XXXIII p. 394,395
7. Ibid., p. 395
8. Herbert M. Schiller, ed. Autobiography of Major General William F. Smith p.83
9. Bruce Catton, Grant Takes Command Boston, Little, Brown & Co. 1968, p. 150-152
10. Herbert M. Schiller, ed. Autobiography of Major General William F. Smith. p.83
11. George Maharay, The Ever-Changing Leaders and Organization of the Army of the Potomac, p. 130

12. George Meade, The Life and Letters of George Gordon Meade, vol. 2, p. 218
13. Herbert M. Schiller, ed. Autobiography of Major General William F. Smith, p. 84
14. O.R. XXXIII p. 861
15. Herbert M. Schiller, ed. Autobiography of Major General William F. Smith, p. 84
16. O.R. XXXIII p. 1019
17. Herbert M. Schiller, ed. Autobiography of Major General William F. Smith, p. 84
18. Benj. F. Butler, Autobiography and Personal Reminiscences of Major General Benj. F. Butler, Butler's Book, Boston, A.m. Thayer & Co., 1892.p. 127
19. Internet Wikipedia
20. Butler's Book p. 127
21. Ibid. p. 81
22. Ibid
23. Ibid p. 221
24. Ibid p. 222
25. Ibid p. 196-201
26. Internet Wikipedia
27. Butler's Book, p. 205-208
28. Ibid. p. 208
29. Ibid p. 631-633
30. Ibid p. 633,634
31. Ibid p. 769, 770
32. O.R. XXXIII p. 1268

Chapter 22 The Army of the James, March 31-May 16, 1864

33. 2. O.R. XXXIV part 1, p. 12
34. Ibid
35. Herbert M. Schiller, ed. Autobiography of Major General William F. Smith, p.84-85
36. Benj. F. Butler, Butler's Book, p.1053, 1054
37. Ibid. p.1054
38. O.R. XXXIII, p.828
39. Ibid. p.804

40. Ibid. p. 886-887
41. Ibid. p. 859
42. O.R. XXXIV part 1, p. 16
43. O.R.XXXVI part 2, p. 34
44. Benj. F. Butler, Butler's book, App. 33, p. 26
45. O.R. XXXVI part 2, p. 34
46. Ibid p. 35
47. Herbert M. Schiller, ed. Autobiography of Major General William F. Smith, p. 86
48. O.R.XXXVI part 2 p. 776-777
49. Herbert M. Schiller, ed. Autobiography of Major General William F. Smith, p. 87
50. William Farrar Smith, From Chattanooga to Petersburg Under Generals Grant and Butler, Boston, Houghton Mifflin & Co. 1893, p. 194
51. Ibid. p 112-117, 150
52. U.S. Grant, Personal Memoirs of U.S. Grant, vol.2, p. 151-152

Chapter 23 Joining the Army of the Potomac, May 17-June 1, 1864

1. Robert U. Johnson and Clarence C. Buel, Battles and Leaders of the Civil War, vol 4, p 212
2. O.R. XXXVI part 1, p. 43
3. Ibid., p. 141
4. Ibid., p. 177, 178
5. Ibid., p.145
6. Ibid., p. 177
7. Ibid., p.183
8. Ibid., p.204, 234
9. Ibid., p. 245
10. Ibid., p. 261
11. Colonel Vincent J. Esposito, The West Point Atlas of the Civil War, Narrative for Map No. 134
12. Robert U. Johnson and Clarence C. Buel, Battles and Leaders of the Civil War, vol 4, p. 286
13. Ibid
14. Benj. F. Butler, Butler's Book, p.1076, Appendix No. 63
15. Ibid., p. 115

16. Ibid., p. 287
17. Ibid., p. 319
18. Ibid., p. 285
19. Colonel Vincent J. Esposito, The West Point Atlas of the Civil War, Narrative for Map 136
20. Robert U. Johnson and Clarence C. Buel, Battles and Leaders of the Civil War, vol 4, p. 323
21. Herbert M. Schiller, ed. Autobiography of Major General William F. Smith, p 91
22. General Andrew A. Humphreys, The Virginia Campaign 1864-1865, p.172-173
23. George S. Maharay, Vermont Hero, Major General George J. Stannard, p. 193
24. General Andrew A. Humphreys, The Virginia Campaign 1864-1865, p.172-173
25. George S. Maharay, Vermont Hero, Major General George J. Stannard, p. 193
26. Herbert M. Schiller, ed. Autobiography of Major General William F. Smith, p. 82
27. Louis J. Baltz III, The Battle of Cold Harbor, Lynchburg, Va., H. Howard, Inc. 1994, p. 186

Chapter 24 The Battle of Cold Harbor, June 1-3, 1864

1. O.R. XXXVI part 3, p. 410
2. Ibid., p. 285, 319
3. Ibid., p. 506, 512
4. Ibid., p. 552, 563
5. Ibid., p. 466
6. Herbert M. Schiller, ed. Autobiography on Major General William F. Smith, p. 92
7. O.R. XXXVI part 3, p. 467
8. Ibid., p. 507
9. Ibid., p. 477
10. Herbert M. Schiller, ed. Autobiography on Major General William F. Smith, p. 92
11. O.R. XXXVI part 3, p.467, 468
12. Ibid., p. 432

13. Ibid., p. 505

14. Ibid

15. Ibid., p. 458

16. Ibid., p. 555

17. Ibid., p.553

18. Ibid., p. 556

19. Ibid., p. 570

20. Ibid., p. 479

21. Herbert M. Schiller, ed. Autobiography on Major General William F. Smith,, p 92

22. General Andrew A. Humphreys, The Virginia Campaign, 1864,-1865, p. 75,76

23. Herbert M. Schiller, ed. Autobiography on Major General William F. Smith, p.93

24. General Andrew A. Humphreys, The Virginia Campaign, 1864,-1865, p. 182

25. Ibid

26. O.R.L.I p. 1255

27. Colonel Vincent J. Esposito, The West Point Atlas of the Civil War, Narrative for Map No. 136

28. O.R. XXXVI, part 3, p.526

29. Ibid., p. 544

30. General Andrew A. Humphreys, The Virginia Campaign, 1864,-1865 p. 186

31. O.R. XXXVI, part 3, p.553

32. Ibid., p. 531

33. Ibid., p. 538

34. Ibid., p.539

35. Herbert M. Schiller, ed. Autobiography on Major General William F. Smith, p.94

36. O.R. XXXVI, part 3, 526

37. Ibid., p. 528

38. U.S. Grant, Personal Memoirs of U.S. Grant, vol 2, p.276

39. George Meade, The Life and letters of George Gordon Meade, vol. 2, p. 200

40. Ibid., p. 201

41. Herbert M. Schiller, ed. Autobiography on Major General William F. Smith, p. 94

Chapter 25 The Attack at Petersburg, June 14-15, 1864 (Until 5:00 P.M. June 15)

1. O.R. XXXVI part 3, p. 745, 748
2. General Andrew Humphreys, The Virginia Campaign p. 213
3. Ibid footnote
4. O.R. XXXVI part 3 p. 755
5. Benj. F. Butler, Butler's Book, p. 685
6. U.S. Grant, Personal Memoirs of U.S. Grant, vol. 2, p.293
7. O.R. XXXVI part 2, p. 287-288
8. Ibid
9. Ibid., p. 398-399
10. Benj. F. Butler, Butler's Book, p. 687-689
11. O.R. XXXVI part 3, p. 709
12. Ibid., p. 715-716
13. O.R. XL part 2, p. 17
14. Ibid., p. 44
15. Ibid., p. 41
16. Ibid., p. 36
17. William Farrar Smith, From Chattanooga to Petersburg Under Generals Grant and Butler, p. 22, 23
18. Herbert M. Schiller, ed., Autobiography of Major General William F. Smith, p. 102 note 61
19. Benj. F. Butler, Butler's Book, p. 587
20. Herbert M. Schiller, ed., Autobiography of Major General William F. Smith, p.100
21. Colonel Vincent J. Esposito, The West Point Atlas of the Civil War, Narrative for Map No. 138
22. William Farrar Smith, From Chattanooga to Petersburg Under Generals Grant and Butler, p.23
23. Herbert M. Schiller, ed., Autobiography of Major General William F. Smith, p.101,
24. Ibid., p. 101
25. Ibid., p. 140
26. Ibid., p. 141
27. Edward G. Longacre, Army of Amateurs, Mechanicsburg, Pa.1997. p. 148

28. Herbert M. Schiller, ed., Autobiography of Major General William F. Smith, p.102

Chapter 26 Petersburg: The Controversial Phase of the Attack, June 15, 1864

1. Benj. F. Butler, Butler's Book, p. 685
2. Herbert M. Schiller, ed. Autobiography of Major General William F. Smith, p. 101
3. O.R. XL part 2, p. 38
4. Ibid., p.83
5. Ibid., p. 49
6. Ibid., p. 74
7. Ibid., p. 79
8. Ibid., p. 83
9. Herbert M. Schiller, ed. Autobiography of Major General William F. Smith p. 41
10. General Andrew A. Humphreys, The Virginia Campaign 1864-1865, 1078
11. General Andrew A. Humphreys, The Virginia Campaign 1864-1865, p.212
12. Herbert M. Schiller, ed. Autobiography of Major General William F. Smith, p. 94
13. Ibid., p. 101-102
14. General Andrew A. Humphreys, The Virginia Campaign 1864-1865, p. 207
15. U.S. Grant, Personal Memoirs of U. S. Grant, vol. 2, p 58
16. Benj. F. Butler, Butler's Book, P. 686
17. O.R. XV part 2 p. 58
18. Ibid., part 1, p.305
19. Ibid., p. 304
20. William Farrar Smith, From Chattanooga to Petersburg Under Generals Grant and Butler, p. 190-191
21. Ibid., p. 23
22. Ibid., p. 24
23. O.R. XL part 2, p. 83
24. Ibid
25. Ibid

26. Herbert M. Schiller, ed. Autobiography of Major General William F. Smith, p. 105
27. O.R. part 1, p. 317
28. Ibid., part 2, p. 83

Chapter 27 The Initial Reactions to the Battle of June 15, 1864

1. O.R. XL part 1, p.305
2. Ibid., p. 805
3. Ibid., p. 84
4. Ibid., p. 21
5. Ibid., p. 305
6. George Meade, The Life and Letters of George Gordon Meade, vol.2, p.204
7. O.R. XL part 1 p. 307
8. George Meade, The Life and Letters of George Gordon Meade, vol. 2, p. 205
9. O.R. XL part 2, p. 86
10. William Farrar Smith, From Chattanooga to Petersburg Under Generals Grant and Butler, p. 27
11. O.R. XL part 2 p. 116
12. Ibid., p. 318
13. Ibid., p. 314
14. Ibid., p. 315
15. Ibid., p. 316
16. William Farrar Smith, From Chattanooga to Petersburg Under Generals Grant and Butler, p. 126

Chapter 28 The Environment of June and July, 1864

1. William Farrar Smith, From Chattanooga to Petersburg Under Generals Grant and Butler, p.80
2. Ibid
3. Benj. F. Butler, Butler's Book, p. 694
4. Appendix 4
5. Ibid
6. O.R. XL part 2, p. 683
7. Benj. F. Butler, Butler's Book, p. 688

8. Ibid
9. O.R. XL part 2, p. 100
10. Ibid p. 130, 131, 143-145
11. O.R. XL part 2, p. 266
12. William Farrar Smith, From Chattanooga to Petersburg Under Generals Grant and Butler, p. 156
13. Ibid., p. 157, 186-188
14. Ibid., p. 179, 189
15. Herbert M. Schiller ed. Autobiography of Major General William F. Smith, p. 109
16. Ibid., p. 109-110
17. William Farrar Smith, From Chattanooga to Petersburg Under Generals Grant and Butler, p. 175

Chapter 29 General Order No. 225

1. O.R. XL part 2, p. 558
2. Ibid
3. Ibid., p. 598
4. Ibid
5. Ibid., part 3, p.31
6. Ibid., p.69
7. Ibid., p.59
8. William Farrar Smith, From Chattanooga to Petersburg Under Generals Grant and Butler p. 189
9. O.R. XL part 3 p. 122
10. Ibid
11. Mark A. Snell, From First to Last, The Life of Major General William B. Franklin, p. 330-331
12. Ibid p. 325
13. O.R. XL part 2, p. 594
14. Ibid., p 595
15. O.R. XLI part 1, p. 88
16. Mark A. Snell, From First to Last, The Life of Major General William B. Franklin, p. 325
17. Herbert M. Schiller, ed. Autobiography of Major General William F. Smith p. 111
18. Ibid., p.112

19. O.R. XXXVI part 1, p. 201, 202
20. Robert U. Johnson and Clarence C. Buel, Battles and Leaders of the Civil War, vol. 4, p. 228
21. Herbert M. Schiller, ed. Autobiography of Major General William F. Smith, p. 114
22. Appendix 4
23. Herbert M. Schiller, ed. Autobiography of Major General William F. Smith, p. 115, 117

Chapter 30 Relieved in Disgrace

1. George Meade, The Life and Letters of George Gordon Meade, vol. 2, p. 214
2. William Farrar Smith, From Chattanooga to Petersburg Under Generals Grant and Butler, p. 175-176
3. Ibid., p. 176, 177
4. Ibid
5. Herbert M. Schiller, ed. Autobiography of Major General William F. Smith, p. 116
6. James Harrison Wilson, Major General USV, Heroes of the Great Conflict, Life and Services of William Farrar Smith, Major General United States Volunteer in the Civil War, p. 46
7. William Farrar Smith, From Chattanooga to Petersburg Under Generals Grant and Butler, p. 178
8. Ibid., p. 58, 59
9. James Harrison Wilson, Major General USV, Heroes of the Great Conflict, Life and Services of William Farrar Smith, Major General United States Volunteer in the Civil War, p. 42
10. Mark A. Snell, From First to Last, The Life of Major General William B. Franklin, p.332
11. William Farrar Smith, From Chattanooga to Petersburg Under Generals Grant and Butler, p. 191
12. Ibid., p. 43
13. Ibid., p. 52
14. Benj. F. Butler, Butler's Book, p. 698
15. Ibid., p. 696
16. Ibid., p. 699, 700
17. Ibid., p. 698

18. Appendix 4
19. William Farrar Smith, From Chattanooga to Petersburg Under Generals Grant and Butler p. 46

Chapter 31 The End of the War and the Postbellum Period

1. Major General William F. Smith, Internet
2. James Harrison Wilson, Major General USV, Heroes of the Great Conflict, Life and Services of William Farrar Smith, Major General United States Volunteer in the Civil War, p. 48
3. Benjamin Franklin Butler, Politician Wikipedia, Internet
4. Vermont Born Generals, Vermont in the Civil War, Internet
5. William Farrar Smith, From Chattanooga to Petersburg Under Generals Grant and Butler, p. 55, 56
6. Herbert M. Schiller, ed. Autobiography of Major General William F. Smith p. 149
7. James Harrison Wilson, Major General USV, Heroes of the Great Conflict, Life and Services of William Farrar Smith, Major General United States Volunteer in the Civil War, p 49
8. Ibid
9. Herbert M. Schiller, ed. Autobiography of Major General William F. Smith p. 141-155
10. Ibid p. xxiv
11. James Harrison Wilson, Major General USV, Heroes of the Great Conflict, Life and Services of William Farrar Smith, Major General United States Volunteer in the Civil War, p. 47-48
12. William F. Smith, Report of a Board of Officers, Internet
13. James Harrison Wilson, Major General USV, Heroes of the Great Conflict, Life and Services of William Farrar Smith, Major General United States Volunteer in the Civil War, p 26
14. N.Y. Times, The Last Sad Tributes, General Hancock's Obituary, February 18, 1886, Internet
15. Fitz John Porter Funeral, N.Y. Times May 22, 1901, Internet
16. Arlington Cemetery.net/wfsmith

BIBLIOGRAPHY

Baltz, Louis J, The Battle of Cold Harbor, Lynchburg, Va. H. Howard, Inc. 1994

Benedict, George G. Vermont in the Civil War, 2 Volumes. Burlington, Vermont, The Free Press, 1886-1888

Butler, Benjamin F. Autobiography and Personal Reminiscences of Major General Benj. F. Butler, Butler's Book, A.M. Thayer & Co. 1892

Catton, Bruce, the Coming Fury, New York, Doubleday and Company, 1961

Coffin, Charles Carleton, Four Years of Fighting, Boston, Mass. Tichenor and Fields. 1866

Crafts, W.A., The Southern Rebellion being a History of the United States from the Commencement of President Buchanan's Administration through the War of the Suppression of the Rebellion, 2 Volumes, Boston, Samuel Walker and Co. 1868,

Crockett, Walter H., the History of Vermont, Volume III, New York, the Century History Company, 1921

Dowdey, Clifford and Louis Manaris, The Wartime Papers of Robert E. Lee, New York, The DeCapo Press 1961

Dutcher, L.L., A.M., The History of St. Albans, Vermont, St. Albans, Vermont, Stephen E. Royce, 1872

Esposito, Colonel Vincent J. The West Point Atlas of the Civil War, New York, Frederick A. Praeger, 1962

Fairchild, Charles Bryant, History of the 27th Regiment Volunteers, Binghamton, New York, 1888

Furgurson, Ernest B., Not War But Murder Cold Harbor 1864, New York, Alfred A. Knopf, 2000

Goodwin, Doris Kearns, Team of Rivals, New York, Simon and Schuster, 2005

Grant, U.S. Personal Memoirs of U.S, Grant, 2 Volumes, New York, Charles Webster and Son, 1885

Hardie, James Allen, Memoir of James Allen Hardie, Inspector General, United States Army, Washington, D.C. Kessenger Publishing, Legacy Reprints, Originally printed 1877

Humphreys, General Andrew A. The Virginia Campaign, 1864-1865. New York, The deCapo Press, 1995

Johnson, Robert U. and Clarence C. Buel, Battles and leaders of the Civil War, 4 Volumes, New York, The Century Company, 1884-1887

Joint Committee on the Conduct of the War, Part 1, Report of, Washington, D.C., Government Printing Office, 1863

Longstreet, General James, From Manassas to Appomattox, New York The DeCapo Press, reprint 1992

Maharay, George S, The Ever-Changing Leaders and Organization of the Army of the Potomac, New York. iUniverse, 2010

Vermont Hero, Major General George J. Stannard, Shippensburg, Pa. White Mane books 2001

Masarek, John E. Commander of All Lincoln's Armies, Life of Henry W. Halleck, Cambridge, Mass. Belknap Press, 2004

McClellan, Major General George B. Report of the Organization of the Army of the Potomac and its Campaigns in Virginia and Maryland, House of Representatives, 38th. Congress, 1st.Session, Executive Document No. 15, Washington, D.C., Government Printing Office, 1864

McClure, Alexander Kelly, Annals of the Civil War, New York, The DeCapo Press reprint 1994

Meade, George G. editor, The Life and Letters of George Gordon Meade, 2 Vol., New York, Charles Scribner and Son, 1914

Murfin, James, The Gleam of Bayonets, New York, Thomas Youseloff, 1968

Palfrey, Francis A., Campaigns of the Civil War, The Antietam and Fredericksburg New York, Charles Scribner and Sons, 1882,

Peck, Theodore s., Revised Roster of Vermont Volunteers Who Served in the Army or the Navy of the United States During the War of the Rebellion, Montpelier, Vermont, Wachtman Company, 1872

Pratt, Fletcher, Stanton, Lincoln's Secretary of War, New York, W.W. Norton and Company, 1953

Rhea, Gordon C., Cold Harbor Grant and Lee May 26-June 3, 164, Baton Rouge, Louisiana State University Press

Schiller, Herbert M. ed., Autobiography of Major General William F. Smith, Dayton, Ohio. Morningside House, 1990

Sears, Stephen W. Controversies and Commanders, Dispatches From the Army of the Potomac, Boston, Houghton Mifflin, 1999

George B. McClellan, the Young Napoleon, New York, Tichenor and Fields, 1988

Landscape Turned Red, New Haven, Ct., Tichenor and Field 1983

Smith, General William F, Diary Vermont Historical Society

From Chattanooga to Petersburg Under Generals Grant and Butler, Boston, Houghton Mifflin & co. 1893

Snell, Mark A., From First to Last, The Life of Major General William B. Franklin, New York, Fordham University Press, 2002

Thomas, Benjamin P. Abraham Lincoln, New York, Alfred A. Knopf. 1952

Thomas, Emory, Robert E. Lee, New York, W.W. Morton and Company, 1995

War Department, War of the Rebellion, Official Records of the Union and Confederate Armies (O.R.s) 138 Volumes, Washington, D.C. Government Printing Office 1880-1901

Warner, Ezra J. Generals in Blue, Baton Rouge, La., Louisiana University Press, 1964

Webb, Alexander, Campaigns of the Civil War, The Peninsula, New York, Charles Scribner Sons, 1881

Westervelt, William B. edited by George S. Maharay, Lights and Shadows of Army life, Shippensburg, Pa. The Burd Street Press 1998

Williams, T. Harry, Lincoln and His Generals, New York, Alfred A. Knopf, 1952

Wilson, Major General U.S.V., James Harrison, Heroes of the Great Conflict. The Life and Services of William Farrar Smith, Major General, United States Volunteer in the Civil War, Wilmington, Delaware, The John Rogers Press, 1904

Internet

Arlington National Cemetery net.wfsmith

Major General Benjamin F. Butler, Wikipedia

Civil War Generals from West Point, Internet

Cullum, George W. Biographical Report of the Officers and Graduates of the United States Military Academy at West Point, New York, since its establishment in 1802, Internet

N.Y. Times, The Last Sad Tribute, General Hancock's Obituary, February 18, 1886

Fitz John Porter Funeral, N.Y. Times, May 22, 1901

Major General Fitz John Porter

Major General William F. Smith

William F. Smith, Report of a Board of Officers

Tyler, John, Presidents and Vice Presidents of the United States. Internet

Vermont Born Generals, Vermont in the Civil War

INDEX